THE LITERATURE OF POLITICAL SCIENCE

A guide for students, librarians and teachers

THE LITERATURE OF
POLITICAL
SCIENCE

A Guide for Students,
Librarians and Teachers

CLIFTON BROCK

R. R. Bowker Company / New York, London 1969

Published by R. R. Bowker Company
(A XEROX COMPANY)
1180 Avenue of the Americas, New York, N.Y. 10036

Copyright © 1969 Xerox Corporation
All Rights Reserved.

Standard Book Number: 8352–0220–8
Library of Congress Catalog Card Number: 79–79426

Manufactured in the United States of America

To My Parents
and to Eunice
Cliff, Doug and Melinda

Contents

List of Illustrations

Preface

There is considerable evidence that today students are using libraries more and liking it less. This situation apparently results from a combination of factors: stiffer course requirements, brighter students, greater emphasis on independent study and research, and increasingly larger and complex libraries.

Very little is being done, however, to facilitate student use of libraries. Few libraries go much further toward initiating students into their mysteries than the typical one-hour "library tour" during freshman orientation. Such efforts are largely a waste of time, since the students are far more interested in checking out their fellow tourists of the opposite sex than in learning how to check out books. In his classes, of course, the student will receive many reading lists or syllabi, plus other more or less authoritarian suggestions, which direct him to specific books, periodical articles, and other library materials. He is far less likely to receive instruction on bibliographical sources and research procedures which would help him to exploit library resources on his own, and this is the type of knowledge which becomes relevant when he has to write term papers or theses and research a subject on his own.

This guide is intended primarily for the undergraduate major and beginning graduate student as an introduction to library materials and research methods in political science. It is not meant for the advanced specialist, whose research in his own area will have carried him far beyond its modest limits. The hope here is to supplement the specific guidance which the student will receive from instructors in the literature of their respective specialties by attempting to provide some "methodological" leads which he may follow up as inclination, curiosity or need move him.

Libraries vary greatly in terms of size and organization, and no general guide will fit the specific library environment within which each student must work. The setting for this guide was a large university library with substantial holdings of political science materials, and to some extent its content and structure reflect this setting. Students may need to make some adjustments in using it in their own library situations. The reference librarians in each institution can facilitate such adjustments. Few of them will be specialists in political science, but they will know the resources of their own library, and they can be of considerable assistance.

PART A: *Information Sources and How to Use Them*

Chapter 1

The Literature of
Political Science

Every student who takes "Poli Sci 1" learns that Aristotle was the first political scientist. He may not have been, of course. The Chinese can make a pretty good case for Lao Tzu, who preceded the great Greek by a couple of centuries. International one-up-man-ship aside, political science literature goes back a long way, and it has grown to staggering proportions since students swapped papyri on Plato's lectures.

Estimating the amount of published literature relating to political science—in books, periodicals, and other formats—is a hopeless business. The data is incomplete, to use a phrase familiar to every present-day political science student. We can only vaguely delineate the parameters, etc. We do know, however, that the Library of Congress has over half-a-million books in its "J," or Political Science, classification. The *International Bibliography of Political Science* now records over 4,200 articles appearing each year in approximately 1,500 journals in a score of languages. Mix all this with a few thousand newspapers, add a million or so government documents, and you have a jungle of printed matter.

And this is only a modest beginning. Political science has gone "interdisciplinary" in a big way. A graduate student, bedevilled by the necessity to keep up with developments in several fields, once observed sourly that "Political Science is a brazen hussy, sired by History out of Philosophy, who ran away at an early age to marry

Sociology, consort bigamously with Psychology, flirting all the while with Statistics, and throwing herself unashamedly at Systems Theory, Cybernetics, and any other bastard discipline which comes down the pike." Such academic nymphomania forces the present generation of students to range far and wide throughout the stacks in search of materials which libraries have classified in subjects other than "Political Science."

In recent years these problems have been compounded by two other trends within the discipline. Before World War II political science could be accused, with considerable justice, of Western provincialism. "Comparative government" was not really comparative, and its geographical scope did not extend much beyond North America and Europe. But the spectacular growth of "area studies" programs in American universities, and particularly within political science departments, now forces students to search for materials from many countries, sometimes in exotic languages or in translation.

On top of this, a strong "quantitative" trend, largely a spinoff from the behavioral movement of the 1950's, is running through the discipline. Thirty years ago the student beginning a piece of research spoke of "searching the literature." Today he is more likely to talk of "gathering data," and the data he gathers—or struggles to gather—ranges far beyond "literature." The political scientist of the last generation, studying the politics of the Gold Coast, might have been content with the London *Times* and a few publications of the British Colonial Office. Today his successor wants to know the world market price of cocoa, the amount and kinds of U.S. economic assistance to Ghana, the tribal distribution of population, plus access to any relevant survey research done in Ghana in order to exploit it for his own purposes through secondary analysis.

The literature of political science, moreover, is far less susceptible to the "obsolescence" which is found in many disciplines in the natural and physical sciences. It is said that no physics student reads anything written more than two or three years ago. With the exception of political philosophy, most segments of political science do show an obsolescence factor, but it does not approach the happy situation of physics. "Political science," Heinz Eulau has noted in this connection, "carries the burden of both past and future. It is, of necessity, a historical discipline, and, of equal necessity, a predictive science."[1] Professor Eulau failed to add that professors at least have the advantage of being able to specialize and restrict their burden to a narrow segment of the discipline. David Easton can make a reputation arguing that precisely what Aristotle had to say about the sixth cause of revolutions does not matter much, but woe unto one of his Chicago students who takes him seriously, then walks into an oral examination to find Professor Leo Strauss sitting there.

There are many other trends running through the literature of political science which surface in the form of hair-rending frustration for students on their excursions into the library.[2] What can be done to overcome or at least to mitigate these problems? Professor Alfred de Grazia has proposed one solution. Noting the "increasing bibliographic frustration" among social scientists, and the obvious incapacity of traditional library methods of manual control to cope with a burgeoning and complex literature, he urges the application of computer technology. "The gentle lady who gives you your library book," de Grazia predicts, "may soon be as rare as 'pop and mom's' corner grocery store. The reason is the same; just as the chain store and supermarket have taken over food supply and distribution functions, new forms of organization may soon supplant the tradtional library system and the library research techniques used by present-day scholars and librarians."[3]

Much has been written in recent years about a utopia in which the student need only sit at his desk, push a button, and there appears on the Batscreen any book, article, or other reference he has commanded. It will come. It, or something close to it, has to come if learning, teaching and research are not to grind to a halt under a mass of paper. But utopia, by definition, lies somewhere in the future. The student reading this old-fashioned piece of print from a pre-McLuhanesque era will not see it, at least not in his next few

[1] Eulau, Heinz, "Political Science." *In* Carl M. White, ed. *Sources of Information in the Social Sciences; a guide to the literature.* Totowa, N.J.: Bedminster Press, 1964, p. 358.

[2] For a more technical and dreary exposition, see the present author's article entitled "Political Science" in the April, 1967, issue of *Library Trends.*

[3] de Grazia, Alfred. "Rationalizing the Intake of Information," *American Behavioral Scientist,* (September, 1960), p. 36.

years as a student. During his time the gentle lady still will be there, and perhaps the best he can hope for is that she becomes a little less old and a little better looking.

It must be said to Professor de Grazia's credit, however, that he has done more than complain about the past and present and call for the computer. In political science literature, he has taken at least an initial step, discussed in Chapter III, toward his utopia.

What can be done, however, while we wait for the machine? As noted in the Preface, libraries have done too little in teaching students to exploit their resources, even through the inadequate manual methods of bibliographic control presently available. The indictment can be carried further: neither libraries, nor professors, nor students themselves have done enough.

A generation ago, in political science departments which offered a course labelled "Methodology," the course consisted largely of teaching students how to find their way through the literature of the discipline. Though many more "Methodology" or "Research Methods" courses are offered today, they focus on sampling procedures, questionnaire design, the philosophical-logical-epistemological underpinnings of scientific method, or on how to feed data into the computer. It is a rare and sparsely-attended course, perhaps taught by some older professor left in the backwash of the behavioral revolution, which deals with such things as "bibliography." The new methodological knowledge is essential, of course, to the professional baggage of any modern political scientist. In making room for it, however, political science departments have thrown away some old clothes which, if no longer fashionable, still retain some usefulness.

This neglect on the part of libraries and professors leaves the student in a sort of limbo between the two, forced into the first (along with hordes of his fellows in other disciplines) by the demands of the second, and prepared for his ordeal by neither. All of which throws the student back largely on his own initiative, ingenuity, and persistence.

While passing out low grades, it may as well be said, at the risk of losing readers, that many students exhibit little of these virtues in using libraries. In the author's experience, a surprising number of them do better than their elders have a right to expect, simply because they must in the interest of academic survival. But many approach the library infrequently and with marked reluctance, driven into Siberia at the last minute in order to complete an assignment, planning to get out quickly to meet a late date, only to be astounded and frustrated at the amount of dogged digging required to find what they need, frequently not finding it, emerging with a poorly-done paper, and vowing never to return.

Chapter 2

Beginning a
Literature Search

Unscientific, non-random surveys indicate that most political science students go to the library looking for one or more of the following:

(1) a specific book, usually one which an instructor has suggested they might do well to read.

(2) sources of information—in book, periodical or whatever form—on some subject for purposes of a term paper, thesis, or other research project.

Probably the best place to begin a literature search is not in the library at all, but in the office of whatever professor specializes in the subject the student wishes to research. The resident expert on political parties will know the literature of this field far better than any reference librarian, and ten minutes with him will save hours in the library. Professors are busy people, however, and frequently off in Washington or elsewhere consulting or researching, thus this informal method of literature searching may not be feasible.

THE CARD CATALOG

In such cases the logical starting point for a search, whether for a specific book or for "subject" information, is the library's card catalog. Though its format may vary slightly in different libraries, normally the catalog will contain cards, arranged alphabetically, for all books and periodicals in the library. There will be at least two or three, and usually five or six, cards for each book in the library's collection:

(1) The *author* card, with the author's name appearing in black type on the top line of the card.

(2) The *title* card; here the title of the book will be on the top line.

(3) The *subject* card. The subject of the book normally appears in red type on the top line; there are usually two or three subject cards for each book.

In looking for a specific book, you usually will know in advance the author or title and would check the appropriate alphabetical section of the catalog. For Almond and Verba's *The Civic Culture,* cards may be located easily under "Almond, Gabriel" in the "A" drawers of the catalog, in the "V" drawers under "Verba, Sidney" or in the "C's" under "Civic Culture."

The "call numbers" in the upper left corner of each card will be the essential information needed, along with author and title, for obtaining the book. In library jargon, these call numbers are "classification numbers," and in most guides of this nature it is traditional at this point to launch into an esoteric explanation of classification schemes. The finer points of "Dewey" or the "Library of Congress" classification systems may intrigue students in the library school, but they are not going to do much for political science students. Just copy down the call number (correctly, otherwise you will waste a half-hour) and don't worry about what it means.

The student should have little trouble locating call numbers through the author or title approaches. Getting hold of the book itself may be another matter. The probability is fairly high that it will have been checked out by someone else, lost, or stolen by a fellow student. This may not be an altogether negative circumstance, however. Professors have had the same experience, and if the matter is timed correctly and put to them properly, they may buy it as an excuse for not reading assigned books.

The student making a "subject" approach—looking for books on some particular subject—may have some difficulty in using the card catalog. The problem will be to find which "subject headings" to look under. Take, for example, the subject which is variously denoted by the terms "pressure groups," "lobbies," or "interest groups." If you look in the "I" section of the catalog under "Interest groups," in most libraries you will find no subject cards. This does not mean that the library has no books on interest groups, but means that it uses some other subject heading to designate them. By switching to the "P" drawers and looking under the heading "Pressure groups," you should find cards with this heading in red type, each card indicating a different book on pressure groups. Filed after these cards you may also find a "cross reference" card reading simply: "Pressure groups, see also Lobbying." Under the heading "Lobbying" you would find other cards, some designating the same books found earlier under "Pressure groups," but there should be new cards indicating additional books not found earlier.

This example illustrates two facets or problems in the subject approach to the card catalog:

(1) Frequently, it is necessary to guess at subject headings and try several possibilities.

(2) The "cross reference" cards will lead you from one subject heading to others which designate similar books.

In many cases the "title cards" will help in pinning down the appropriate subject heading. In the above example, there were no subject cards under "Interest groups," but there is a card (see illustration on the following page) with black type on the top line reading: "Interest groups in American society." This is the title card for a book by Harmon Zeigler. Near the bottom of the card are listed the subject headings used for this book: "1. Pressure groups," and "2. Representative government and representation—U.S." From this you would know to look under the subject heading "Pressure groups" for books on interest groups.

The same procedure can be followed with author cards. Suppose you are looking for books on the behavioral approach to political science. You probably will find no subject cards under "Behavioralism" or "Political behavior." Perhaps you know, however, that Heinz Eulau has written a book on this subject. Looking under "Eulau, Heinz" in the catalog, you may find an author card for his book, *The Behavioral Persuasion in Politics*. Near the bottom of the card you will find the note: "1. Political psychology" and under the subject heading "Political psychology" you should find books dealing with the behavioral approach to political science.

323
Z45i
Zeigler, Harmon.
    Interest groups in American society. Englewood Cliffs,
N. J., Prentice-Hall ₍1964₎

      viii, 343 p. 22 cm.

      Bibliographical footnotes.

Pressure groups

323
Z45i
Zeigler, Harmon.
    Interest groups in American society. Englewood Cliffs,
N. J., Prentice-Hall ₍1964₎

      viii, 343 p. 22 cm.

      Bibliographical footnotes.

Representative government and representation
-U. S.

323
Z45i
Zeigler, Harmon.
    Interest groups in American society. Englewood Cliffs,
N. J., Prentice-Hall ₍1964₎

      viii, 343 p. 22 cm.

      Bibliographical footnotes.

Interest groups in American society

323
Z45i
Zeigler, Harmon.
    Interest groups in American society. Englewood Cliffs,
N. J., Prentice-Hall ₍1964₎

      viii, 343 p. 22 cm.

      Bibliographical footnotes.

    1. Pressure groups. 2. Representative government and representa-
tion—U. S.   ɪ. Title.

JK1118.Z4   323   64—10841

Library of Congress   ₍67J5₎

Library Catalog Cards

These examples illustrate a major problem in the subject approach to the card catalog: subject headings frequently are out-of-date and fail to keep up with the development of a discipline. In his classes, for example, the student will learn that the term "pressure group" is loaded, indicating an unscientific and non-objective mind; the political scientist is supposed to prefer the more neutral terms "interest groups" or "voluntary associations." Take the case of the student who reads Almond and Coleman's *The Politics of Developing Areas* and wants to follow up on their concept of "political articulation." He will find no subject cards under "Political articulation." Under the subject heading "Articulations," it is likely he will find a cross reference reading: "See Joints." Under "Joints" he may find several books on anatomy. While this may stimulate the systems theorist into a brilliant piece of analogical research, it is not likely to help most students.

So long as the subject is fairly "concrete," there should be no major problems in the subject approach to the card catalog, but library subject cataloging has failed to maintain pace with the development of abstract concepts in the various disciplines. The fault does not lie entirely with librarians. Part of the problem stems from the fact that no young social scientist is considered to have "arrived" until he has developed and written about an entirely new concept of his own which no one else can understand.

Another problem lies in the small number of subject headings for a given book provided by library catalogs. Usually there are no more than two or three for each book, and this is grossly inadequate in most cases. George Sabine's opus on political theory, for example, will be listed only under the single heading: "Political science-History." The fact that he deals with a few hundred odd political philosophers from Plato through Stalin (?) will not be reflected in the card catalog. Ideally, perhaps we should have a subject card for every individual, term, or concept mentioned by an author, in effect reproduce the index to his book in the card catalog. Perhaps in the not too distant future the computers will allow libraries to keep abreast of the development of jargon and also provide detailed subject approaches to books, but until that time the student will have to struggle with the catalog as it is.

There are all sorts of details relating to use of a card catalog, such as filing rules, sub-headings (form and geographical), added entries, contents notes, etc. Library science, no less than political science, has its jargon. In 99 cases out of 100, however, the student can proceed in happy ignorance of such minutiae. If he stumbles over them, he can check with the library staff, whose business it is to know the intricacies of the card catalog, and who are paid, at least in part, to help students use it.

In addition, there are many "how-to-do-it" books offering elementary instruction in using libraries, their card catalogs and other general bibliographical tools. By the time they begin to major in political science, most students will probably have absorbed many of these details. Those who feel a need for review, however, might want to consult:

Downs, Robert B. *How to Do Library Research.* Urbana: Univ. of Illinois Press, 1966.

Hook, Lucyle and Mary V. Gaver. *The Research Paper; gathering library material, organizing and preparing the manuscript.* 3rd ed. Englewood Cliffs, N.J.: Prentice-Hall, 1962.

Chapter 3

Periodical Indexes
and Abstracts

In most cases the student writing a term paper or thesis will find that books alone do not provide sufficient information on his subject. Several possibilities arise:

(1) His topic may be of such recent vintage that no books have yet appeared on the subject. Someone concerned with a presidential election which took place four months ago, for example, would not find it very productive to search the card catalog looking for books on this particular election. Books will appear in due course, but political scientists will allow a decent interval before publication, knowing that otherwise their colleagues will blast them for "premature publication aimed at the mass market."

(2) His topic may be so specialized that it has not been treated adequately in book form. Someone attempting to assess the political impact of U.S. military and economic aid to Ethiopia would need to go far beyond books to produce a suitable paper.

(3) Instructors are likely to look with jaundiced eye on a paper which lists only books in its bibliography and obviously has been patched together from a few secondary sources.

In these, and many other situations, the most productive source of additional information is likely to be periodical articles. Perhaps one other reason for delving into the periodical literature should be mentioned. Many of your professors will have published articles in political science journals. Some of them will be considerate or immodest enough to tell you about them; your problem then will be to work a citation to their articles into your paper. Others will say nothing, but may flunk you if you fail to discover and cite their articles. Thus, there are pragmatic as well as intellectual reasons for learning your way about in periodical literature.

The card catalog will be of no help in this respect. It will contain title and subject cards for periodicals in the library, but will not have subject, author, or title cards for specific articles in these periodicals. Access to the periodical literature of political science is available, however, through various indexes and abstracts. The student probably is familiar with the *Readers' Guide to Periodical Literature,* which indexes articles in about a hundred "popular" magazines such as *Time, Newsweek, New Republic,* etc. Fortunately, the format of the indexes listed below is generally similar to that of the *Reader's Guide,* so there should be little difficulty in using them. By way of review, however, here is a typical reference which might be encountered:

POLITICAL PARTIES—France

> Theories of the French party system under the Third Republic. B. D. Graham. Pol Studies 12:21–32 F '64

Explanation:

POLITICAL PARTIES	Subject heading
France	Sub-heading
Theories of, etc.	Title of article
B. D. Graham	Author of article
Pol Studies	Title of periodical†
12:	Volume of periodical
21–32	Pages on which article appears
F '64	Date of periodical issue

† Periodical titles frequently are abbreviated, but there is usually a complete list at the front of the index.

The differences between a periodical *index* and a periodical *abstract* are significant. An index usually will provide no more information than appears in the example above, and you might spend considerable time running down an article only to find that it is not particularly relevant to your needs. An abstract, however, will go further than an index and give a brief summary of the contents of an article. Most of these abstracts, whether provided by the author of the article himself or written by a professional abstractor, will be descriptive rather than critical. Even so, normally it will be more profitable to start your literature search with a periodical abstract, then switch to an index (which usually lists more articles) if you need to push your search further.

Some indexes and abstracts cover periodical articles only; others include books, documents and other non-periodical literature. Many do not provide complete coverage of all the articles in a given periodical, but will select those judged to be most important.

The subject headings used in periodical indexes and abstracts are similar to those used in library card catalogs for books, and they present much the same problems. Fortunately, those indexes and abstracts which specialize in political science coverage have made a little better adjustment to the changing terminology of the discipline.

The choice of which periodical indexes or abstracts to use will depend upon the subject being researched and the depth to which the student needs to take his literature search. Someone writing a brief term paper in an undergraduate course might want to limit his search to one or two general indexes or abstracts and not get bogged down in more specialized sources. The student with a more serious research problem would have to dig much deeper. In such cases, the optimum search strategy probably would be to start with a specialized abstract or index, provided one is available in his subject area, then supplement it by using more general sources. Hopefully, the descriptions below will provide sufficient information about each index and abstract for you to make appropriate choices.

GENERAL POLITICAL SCIENCE INDEXES AND ABSTRACTS

The indexes and abstracts described in this section are "general" sources, that is, they cover the literature of political science or social science as a whole.

International Political Science Abstracts. Oxford, Eng.: Basil Blackwell, 1951– . Contains 150–200 word abstracts of articles appearing in over 100 English and foreign-language political science journals. All the leading scholarly journals are covered, though not all articles in each journal are abstracted. Published quarterly, with subject and author indexes. Generally, the abstracts appear six to nine months after publication of articles themselves. Prepared by the International Political Science Association in co-operation with the Unesco-sponsored International Committee for Social Sciences Documentation. This is probably the best starting point for most literature searches, though the political historian will want to supplement it by using *Historical Abstracts,* described below.

International Bibliography of Political Science. Chicago: Aldine Publishing Co., 1952–   . An index (no abstracts) to articles appearing in over 1,000 periodicals. Covers all the major and many minor political science journals, though indexing is selective. Also includes books, pamphlets, and some book reviews, as well as important publications in sociology, psychology, and other social science fields. Entries are classified by broad subjects, i.e., "Governmental Processes," "International Relations," etc., with detailed subclassifications. Published annually, with author and subject indexes, under auspices of the International Committee for Social Sciences Documentation. This is the broadest political science index available, and a must for any intensive literature search. Generally two years behind the literature in publication, however, and therefore does not cover very recent material.

Public Affairs Information Service Bulletin. New York: Public Affairs Information Service, 1915–   . A wide-ranging subject index to social science literature, including, but going far beyond, political science and covering selectively over a thousand periodicals as well as books, pamphlets, and some U.S. and foreign government documents. Limited to English-language sources, but covers these on a world-wide basis. Published weekly, thus the most up-to-date index available, with five cumulated issues a year ending with an annual volume.

Social Sciences and Humanities Index. New York: H. W. Wilson, 1907–   . A subject and author index to over 200 major scholarly journals in the social sciences and humanities. Published quarterly, with two-year and five-year cumulations. The political science journals which it covers (approx. 30) are indexed in other sources listed in this guide, but this index still is useful for its complete indexing of all journals covered, its relatively fast coverage and its inclusion of articles in sociology, history, and related disciplines. Until 1965, its title was *International Index.*

Bulletin Analytique de Documentation Politique, Economique et Sociale Contemporaine. Paris: Presses Universitaires de France, 1946– . An index, with brief abstracts, of articles, books, and documents, with emphasis on European journals. Published eight times a year, with an annual subject index, under auspices of the Fondation Nationale des Sciences Politiques. (Don't check this unless you read French.)

Bibliographie der Sozialwissenschaften. Göttingen: Vandenhoeck & Ruprecht, 1905– . An index to the periodical and book literature of the social sciences generally, but with excellent political science coverage. Now issued two to three times a year, with annual author, subject and title indexes. An important source for the student who reads German.

American Political Science Review. Washington: American Political Science Assn., 1906– . From 1906 to 1966 each quarterly issue of the APSR contained a "Selected Articles and Documents" section. This was a classified listing, arranged by broad subjects, of articles appearing in the major English and foreign-language journals, as well as some government documents. This section was discontinued with the December, 1966, issue, and its absence probably will force political scientists to depend more than in the past upon the other indexes and abstracts described in this chapter.

ABC POL SCI; Advance Bibliography of Contents: Political Science and Government. Santa Barbara, Calif.: American Bibliographical Center-Clio Press, 1969– . This is a new "current contents" service, which began publication March, 1969. Published eight times a year, it will reproduce the tables of contents of about 260 journals in political science, public administration, law and related fields. An annual subject index is planned; an author index will appear in each issue and will be cumulated twice a year. An "Article Copying Service" will be available to subscribers, through which copies of any article listed may be ordered at a cost of ten cents per page. The service is designed, in part, "to overcome the information gap caused by the termination of the articles list carried up to a few years ago in the *American Political Science Review.*" Though "current contents" services have been common in physical and natural sciences disciplines, this is the first such service oriented specifically toward political science. If it lives up to the prepublication advertising, and can survive economically, it should be a useful bibliographic resource, particularly for those students and researchers whose direct access to political science journals is limited.

Current Contents: behavioral, social and management sciences. Philadelphia: Institute for Scientific Information, 1969– . Another new service, similar to but broader than *ABC POL SCI,* also scheduled to begin publication in 1969. *Current Contents* will be published weekly and will reproduce the tables of contents to about 700 journals in various social science disciplines, along with an author index and article copying service. Apparently these two services will duplicate each other, at least to some extent, in their coverage of political science journals; the major difference is that *ABC POL SCI* will focus specifically on journals of political science interest, while *Current Contents* will cover many journals from other social and behavioral science fields.

Janda, Kenneth, ed. *Cumulative Index to the American Political Science Review; Volumes 1–57:1906–1963.* Evanston, Ill.: Northwestern Univ. Press, 1964. A computer-produced "keyword" index to over 2,600 articles appearing in the APSR during these years. The articles also are listed alphabetically by author. Though this covers the leading scholarly journal in political science, it is most unlikely that anyone would wish to limit his literature search to a single journal, and thus the index is of limited usefulness.

THE AMERICAN BEHAVIORAL SCIENTIST-UNIVERSAL REFERENCE SYSTEM BIBLIOGRAPHIES

Within the last few years Alfred de Grazia and associates on the *American Behavioral Scientist* have initiated a new program which promises significant improvements in bibliographical control of political science literature. Beginning on a very modest level in 1957, this program has developed through three levels or stages:

(1) *The American Behavioral Scientist.* Beverly Hills, Calif.: Sage Publications, 1957– . Each monthly issue of ABS contains an insert section entitled "New Studies; a guide to recent publications in the social and behavioral sciences." This consists of brief abstracts of articles selected from over 300 journals, plus significant new books. The attempt is to "present each month the best works throughout the whole range of the social and behavioral sciences, with a special emphasis upon methodological works." An excellent "current awareness" source, particularly for its coverage of behavioral and methodological literature in political science, sociology, and related disciplines.

(2) *The ABS Guide to Recent Publications in the Social and Behavioral Sciences.* Beverly Hills, Calif.: Sage Publications, 1965– . This is a cumulation of abstracts appearing in the "New Studies" section of the *American Behavioral Scientist.* The first volume, published in 1965, contained the abstracts which appeared from 1957 through 1964. Annual cumulative volumes have been issued since 1966. The abstracts are listed alphabetically by author, with a subject and methodological index.

(3) *The Universal Reference System.* New York: Metron, Inc., 1967– . In the summer of 1967 the Universal Reference System, founded by de Grazia after terminating his direct association with the *American Behavioral Scientist,* began publishing a series of computer-produced bibliography-indexes covering ten sub-fields of political science. URS is now in the process of publishing basic bibliographical volumes, called Codexes, which cover the significant literature—including periodical articles, books, and documents—of each sub-field. The Codexes are supplemented by "Quarterly Gazettes" bringing coverage up-to-date, with an annual cumulation for each gazette at the end of the year. Initially, the Universal Reference System plans to issue Codexes and "Quarterly Gazettes" in the following subject areas of political science:

International Affairs
Legislative Process, Deliberation, and Decision Making
Administrative Management: Public and Private Bureaucracy
Current Events and Problems of Modern Society
Public Opinion, Mass Behavior and Political Psychology
Law, Jurisprudence, and Judicial Process
Economic Regulation, Business, and Government
Public Policy and the Management of Science
Comparative Government and Cultures
Bibliography of Bibliographies in Political Science, Government
  and Public Policy

In terms of coverage of the literature, or the listing and description of publications, the URS series does not differ significantly from other indexes and abstracts already available. The element in its program which is unique for political science is the indexing. Based upon a classification system developed by de Grazia, it provides subject indexing in greater depth and sophistication than is presently available through library card catalogs or periodical indexes. The inclusion of "methodological" terms in the indexing system, which indicate the various methodological techniques and concepts used by authors of the works cited, should provide a much-needed approach to the literature of political science which is almost entirely absent from traditional library cataloging and indexing.

Though its program is not fully operative as of this writing, in 1965 the Universal Reference System published its first Codex volume, on *International Affairs,* which will serve to illustrate the new approaches it makes possible. The *International Affairs* Codex was produced on IBM 1401/1410 computers and contains citations, annotations and index descriptors to over 3,000 books and articles on international relations. As a bibliography, the volume is unexceptional, being limited largely to standard English-language publications of recent vintage, and practically all of these would be covered in other, though scattered, indexes and bibliographies. There are obvious gaps in coverage. Only three writings on Vietnam are listed in the Codex bibliography; one of these is Bernard Fall's widely-known book, *The Two Vietnams,* and the other two are articles in *Current History.* Even in 1965, a search of other bibliographical sources would have turned up many more significant books and articles on Vietnam.

The index to the URS volume, however, covers 995 pages and provides many more approaches to the literature than conventional indexing systems. While library card catalogs or periodical indexes generally will contain no more than two or three "subject entries" for a book or article, the URS index may carry as many as ten to fifteen, plus the "methodological" index approaches not available in the older, traditional sources. For example, the library card catalog will have only two subject entries—"Political Science-Methodology" and "Communication"—for Karl Deutsch's book, *The Nerves of Government.* The URS *International Affairs* Codex has eleven entries for the same book; seven of these are "topical" or subject entries indicating that the book is about "Power," "Legitimacy," "Interpersonal Communication," etc., while four are methodological entries indicating that Deutsch employs or deals with "Decision Theory and Game Theory," "Scientific Models," "Scientific Communication," and "Stereotypes."

The Universal Reference System program is in an early stage of development, and it is impossible to assess its full value for political science students. Its utility will depend heavily upon how well the descriptors of de Grazia's "Topical and Methodological Index" system fit the needs of students and researchers, and upon the value of "intensive" access to a relatively small body of standard literature. Students may find the URS Codexes and Gazettes somewhat difficult to use at first because their organization and format differ radically from the standard indexes and abstracts; it may be helpful to consult de Grazia's article, "Continuity and Innovation in Reference Retrieval in the Social Sciences: Illustrations from the Universal Reference System," in the February, 1967, issue of *American Behavioral Scientist*.

SPECIALIZED INDEXES AND ABSTRACTS

In addition to the sources described above, which deal more or less directly with political science literature, there are several other indexes which specialize in various sub-fields of political science:

Public Administration Abstracts and Index of Articles. New Delhi: Indian Inst. of Public Admin., 1957– . Indexes articles from a few selected English-language journals relating to public administration. Issued monthly without any cumulations. The coverage is limited, reaching to only a portion of the literature of public administration, but still useful for long abstracts of major articles and some emphasis on administration in developing areas.

International Information Service. Chicago: Lib. of Intl. Relations, 1963– . "A guide to documentary resources, scholarly analyses and significant commentaries on contemporary political, economic and social developments in all parts of the world." Published quarterly, with emphasis more upon factual "current affairs" type sources than upon theoretical writings. Books, articles and documents are listed by broad subject areas, with sections on "International Political and Military Factors," "International Organization and Law," etc. Some coverage of statistical sources.

Index to Periodical Articles, 1950–1964, in the Library of the Royal Institute of International Affairs. 2 vs. Boston: G. K. Hall, 1964. The Library of the Royal Institute of International Affairs, commonly referred to as Chatham House, contains the largest collection of materials on international affairs in Great Britain. These volumes contain photographic reproductions of the Library's card index to articles in some 200 periodicals between 1950 and 1964. Arranged by a special classification system developed by Chatham House. This duplicates other sources, but will contain some articles not indexed elsewhere.

Peace Research Abstracts Journal. Clarkson, Ontario: Canadian Peace Research Inst., 1964– . Contains abstracts from several hundred journals, covering writings on arms control, alliances, decision-making, communication, and related subjects. Abstracts are classified into ten sections, or broad subject areas, with detailed sub-classifications. Each monthly issue covers two or three sections of the classification, providing full coverage roughly on a semi-annual schedule. There are periodic author and subject indexes. A "Coding Manual" explains the classification system and how to use the *Journal.*

Arms Control and Disarmament; a quarterly bibliography with abstracts and annotations. Washington: Govt. Printing Off., 1965– . Each issue contains abstracts of recent books, articles, and other writings on the political, strategic, historical and other aspects of arms control and disarmament. Lists about 2,000 items per year. Abstracts are classified into six broad subject areas. Each issue has an author and subject index which is cumulated into an annual index with the fourth issue of the year. Prepared by the Arms Control and Disarmament Bibliography Section of the Library of Congress through support of the U.S. Arms Control and Disarmament Agency.

Leonard, L. Larry, ed. *Current Thought on Peace and War.* White Plains, N.Y.: Current Thought, Inc., 1960– . "A world affairs digest of literature and research in progress on current international issues." Published twice a year, with each issue containing 500-word abstracts of books, articles, and documents, plus a list of supplementary sources and research in progress. Considerable duplication of other sources, but particularly useful for the long abstracts.

Air University Library Index to Military Periodicals. Maxwell Air Force Base, Ala.: Air Univ. Lib., 1949– . "A subject index to significant articles, news items and editorials appearing in 58 English-language military and aeronautical periodicals not indexed in readily available commercial indexing services." An excellent source for the study of military and strategic affairs. Published quarterly with cumulative annual volumes.

Current Issues; a selected bibliography on subjects of concern to the United Nations. New York: United Nations, 1965–   . A quarterly index of periodical articles on subjects relating to the work of the UN and its specialized agencies. Has a section on "Political and Security Questions." Continues *Monthly List of Selected Articles,* which covered the same ground and was published from 1929 through September, 1963, first by the League of Nations and then by the UN.

Index to Selected Periodicals. Boston: G. K. Hall, 1950–   . A subject and author index to articles on all aspects of Negro life which appear in leading Negro publications (*Crisis, Ebony, Phylon,* etc.) and articles in other journals on the Negro. Published quarterly with annual cumulations. Based on the holdings of the Schomburg Collection of Negro literature and history of the New York Public Library and the Hallie Q. Brown Memorial Library, Central State University, Wilberforce, Ohio. Valuable for anyone working on civil rights subjects.

British Humanities Index. London: The Library Assn., 1915–   . A quarterly subject index, with annual cumulations, to about 300 British periodicals. The title is misleading, since it covers many journals in the social sciences, e.g., *Political Studies, The Economist,* etc. From 1915 to 1961, was published under the title *Subject Index to Periodicals.*

Canadian Periodical Index. Ottawa: Canadian Lib. Assn., 1948–   . A monthly subject and author index to articles in about 90 Canadian periodicals. Cumulated annually, with a 12-year cumulation, covering the years 1948–1959, published in 1962. Indexes *Canadian Public Administration* and several other journals of political science interest.

Index to Latin American Periodicals; humanities and social sciences. Metuchen, N.J.: Scarecrow Press, 1961–   . A subject and author index to articles in about 100 journals published in Latin America. The index, based on holdings of the Pan American Union Library, is issued quarterly and cumulated annually. An eight-volume *Index to Latin American Periodical Literature, 1929–1960* (Boston: G. K. Hall) provides historical coverage in the same area. A must for Latin American specialists.

African Abstracts; quarterly review of articles appearing in current periodicals. London: Intl. African Inst., 1950– . Contains abstracts of articles appearing in about 75 journals, with about 200 abstracts in each issue. Originally, this was primarily a source for anthropologists and linguists, but in recent years coverage has broadened to other disciplines. Arrangement is geographical, with a key number indicating subject of the article; no. 7 is "Government, Administration, Political Studies."

Australian Public Affairs Information Service; a subject index to current literature. Canberra: Commonwealth National Lib., 1945– . A "guide to material on Australian political, economic, social and cultural affairs." Selectively indexes about 150 periodicals published in Australia and elsewhere.

These are the major periodical indexes and abstracts for searching the literature of political science. In addition, however, some periodicals will themselves contain classified lists, if not indexes, to the literature. Probably the most familiar case is the now-defunct "Selected Articles and Documents" section of the *American Political Science Review,* which was mentioned above. To take only one other example at this point, each year the *Journal of Asian Studies* publishes a special issue listing all significant articles, books, etc., published on Asian countries during the preceding year. Most sub-fields of political science have similar journals, though in many cases coverage of the literature is highly selective and inadequate. These journals will be listed and discussed later in the appropriate subject sections of this guide.

INDEXES AND ABSTRACTS IN OTHER DISCIPLINES

Given the interdisciplinary trend which is running in political science, students occasionally will want to—or have to—search the literature of other disciplines, particularly other social science fields. Each of these disciplines has its own bibliographic apparatus, in some cases more extensive and better than that available for political science. Students who are minoring in sociology, psychology or some other field, or who move into these subjects in the course of researching a thesis or paper, may need to explore their bibliographical resources in some depth. Such expeditions are outside the scope of this guide; the most we can do here is indicate some of the major indexing and abstracting tools in other social science disciplines.

Sociological Abstracts. New York: Sociological Abstracts, Inc., 1952– . Carries about 3,300 abstracts per year of articles and books in sociology, and covers all the major sociological journals. Abstracts are classified into 21 subject sections, with sub-classifications. Particularly useful to political scientists for its coverage of the literature of political sociology, public opinion, bureaucracy, and research methodology. Published eight times a year, with an author index in each issue and an annual cumulative author and subject index.

Psychological Abstracts. Washington: American Psychological Assn., 1927– . Generally considered the best abstracting tool in the social sciences. Covers all the significant literature of psychology, carrying over 15,000 abstracts of articles, books, and reports per year. Its coverage of the literature of social psychology, particularly on attitudes and opinions, is most relevant for political scientists. Published monthly, with author and subject indexes in each issue which are cumulated annually. A cumulative subject index covering the years 1927–1960, as well as cumulated author indexes covering 1927–1963, have been published by the G. K. Hall Co.

Historical Abstracts. Santa Barbara, Calif.: American Bibliographic Center, 1955– . Abstracts periodical articles, primarily from historical journals, which deal with all aspects of history during the period from 1775 to 1945. The abstracts are arranged by geographical area and broad topics; the topical section has sub-sections on "international relations" and "political history." Published quarterly with an annual index issue.

America; history and life. Santa Barbara, Calif.: American Bibliographic Center, 1964– . Contains abstracts of articles from about 500 U.S. and Canadian periodicals on American and Canadian history from earliest times to the present. Published three times a year, with an annual index.

Index to Legal Periodicals. New York: H. W. Wilson, 1908– . A subject index to articles in over 250 legal journals. Covers all the "law reviews," which frequently contain articles of political science interest. Published monthly, with annual and three-year cumulations.

Journal of Economic Abstracts. Chicago: American Economic Assn., 1963– . A quarterly journal containing lengthy abstracts of articles in the major economic periodicals, both English and foreign. Supplemented by a five-volume *Index of Economic Journals* (Homewood, Ill.: Irwin, 1961–62) which indexes, but does not abstract, economic articles published from 1886 to 1963.

International Bibliography of Economics. Chicago: Aldine Publishing Co., 1952– . Published under the auspices of the Unesco International Committee for Social Sciences Documentation. An annual classified listing of books and articles in economics. No abstracts. Selectively indexes over a thousand journals and now lists over 7,000 items each year. Supplements the *Journal of Economic Abstracts* by its inclusion of books, as well as articles, and its coverage of foreign-language literature.

Education Index. New York: H. W. Wilson, 1929– . A subject index to articles in about 200 leading education journals. Published monthly with quarterly and annual cumulations. The student researching federal aid to education, or other topics with a government-education relationship, might find leads here not accessible through strictly political science indexes.

Business Periodicals Index. New York: H. W. Wilson, 1958– . A subject index to articles in about 170 business periodicals. Published monthly, cumulated quarterly and annually. The *Industrial Arts Index* provides index coverage of business periodicals from 1913 to 1957. Might be a useful source in researching any subject relating government and business.

Michigan Index to Labor Union Periodicals. Ann Arbor: Bureau of Industrial Relations, Grad. Sch. of Business Admin., Univ. of Michigan, 1960– . "A monthly subject index to materials from a selected list of newspapers and journals published by major labor unions." Covers about 50 publications and issued monthly with annual cumulations.

International Bibliography of Social and Cultural Anthropology. Chicago: Aldine Publishing Co., 1955. An annual subject and author index to the periodical and book literature of anthropology. A companion volume to the Unesco-sponsored *International Bibliography of Political Science.*

Poverty and Human Resources Abstracts. Ann Arbor: Inst. of Labor and Industrial Relations, Univ. of Michigan and Wayne State Univ., 1966– . A bimonthly journal containing long abstracts of articles, books, reports, Congressional publications and other materials on economic, political, and social conditions of the poor.

HOW TO LOCATE PERIODICALS

Locating an article "bibliographically" through the periodical indexes and abstracts described above is, of course, only half the job. Unless he is simply compiling a list of articles, the student will want to locate the periodical itself and read the article.

The library will have a record of which periodicals, and which volumes of a given periodical, are in its collections, though the format of this record varies from library to library. Probably the most prevalent pattern is a "serials catalog" or "periodicals catalog" similar to, but usually filed separately from the general card catalog discussed in Chapter 2. Rather than confuse matters here, however, perhaps it is best to pass this buck on and refer readers to their local librarians.

In this connection, however, the student—if he has not already encountered it—had better be prepared to hear about "the bindery." This is the place where the particular periodical volume he wants seems always to have gone, to return when nobody knows. It will come back, but don't hold your breath.

In some cases, of course, your own library may not subscribe to a particular periodical which you need. See Chapter 18, on "Interlibrary Loan" for leads on how to proceed in such a situation.

NEWSPAPER INDEXES

Unlike periodicals, few newspapers are indexed. While many newspapers maintain a clipping file in their "morgue" which in effect is a subject index, these files generally are not available for public use. There are, however, printed indexes for four major newspapers:

New York Times Index. New York: New York Times, 1851– . A detailed subject index to the *Times,* with reference to date, page, and column where articles appear. Published twice a month and cumulated into annual volumes. Cumulated indexes are currently available for the years 1851 through 1967, with the exception of those for 1907–1912, which are to be reprinted shortly.

Index to the Times. 1906– . London: The Times, 1907– . Indexes material in the London *Times* by date, page, and column. Though much briefer, *Palmer's Index to the Times Newspaper, 1790–June 1941* provides coverage for earlier years.

Subject Index of the Christian Science Monitor. Boston: Christian Science Monitor, 1960– . A monthly subject index with semi-annual and annual cumulations.

Wall Street Journal Index. New York: Dow Jones, 1958– . One section on "Corporate News" indexes articles by company name, the other section on "General News" is a subject index to general articles. Published monthly and cumulated annually.

Canadian News Index. Regina: Univ. of Saskatchewan, 1966– . A biweekly index of Canadian news from 13 of the newspapers published in Canada's 10 provinces.

The indexes listed above can be used as rough guides to the contents of other newspapers. Through the *New York Times Index,* for example, one can establish the date of a given event, say Roosevelt's "quarantine" speech of October 5, 1937, then check the *Chicago Tribune* or any other paper of October 6th and succeeding days for its coverage and interpretation of his speech.

Chapter 4

Book Reviews

Scene: Library reference desk, University of North Carolina.

Time: Five minutes before closing.

Action: Student rushes up to desk, assumes desperate expression, and pleads, "I've got to make a book report for Robson's eight o'clock and haven't read the book. Where can I get a good review?"

Chances are this student is a new boy. Anyone who had been around for a semester already would have checked into the infirmary, taken a trip, anything to avoid the coming confrontation. It is risky business to try to fake out any professor in this manner, and death to try it with this one. He will have read the book—and the book review. ("Robson," for those who are not privileged to know him, is Professor Charles B. Robson of the Political Science Department at the University of North Carolina. It is said that students at Chapel Hill have a "pool," the proceeds of which will go to the student who can find anything in the fields of political theory or comparative politics which he has not read.)

There are, of course, legitimate reasons for wanting book reviews. Often, however, the reviews will not be of much help, being too short, too uncritical, or too skewed in the direction of the reviewer's own pet interests. They are, moreover, rather difficult to locate quickly. For those who want to make the effort, however, there are several possible sources:

Book Review Digest. New York: H. W. Wilson, 1905–   . This is an
    index and digest of book reviews appearing in about 75 American and

English periodicals. Arrangement is alphabetical by author of the book reviewed, with a title and subject index. For each book, brief excerpts or summaries are given from three to four reviews, plus citations to several other reviews. Most of the reviews in the *Digest* appear in general or popular periodicals, and it covers only five or six leading political science journals. Published monthly and cumulated semi-annually and annually.

Book Review Index. Detroit: Gale Research, 1965– . An author index to reviews appearing in over 200 periodicals. Does not give a digest of the reviews, but covers a few more political science journals than the *Book Review Digest* and cites many more reviews. Also, the *Book Review Digest* will list a given book only once and thus may miss some late-appearing reviews in scholarly journals, whereas the *Book Review Index* continues to index reviews whenever they appear. Published monthly, with quarterly and annual cumulations.

Index to Book Reviews in the Humanities. Williamston, Mich.: Phillip Thomson, 1960– . The title is somewhat misleading; though this index stresses history, literature, and other humanistic subjects, it includes many reviews of social science books. Published annually, and indexes almost 700 periodicals.

One other source worth trying is the *International Bibliography of Political Science,* described in Chapter 3, which frequently cites reviews of the books it lists.

So far as political science is concerned, these book review indexes do not give anything approaching complete coverage. None of them, for example, indexes the *Western Political Quarterly,* which has a fairly extensive book review section, and many other important journals are not indexed. If these sources do not pay off sufficiently, the next best thing is to check the political science journals themselves. Most of them will have annual indexes which list the books they have reviewed during the year. The problem will be to pick likely journals. If the book in question has to do with international relations, for example, it may have been reviewed in *World Politics* or *International Affairs.* (There are two journals with the title *International Affairs,* one British and the other Russian. The latter is interesting, but not for objective book reviews.) In all cases, it will save time to know the date the book was published, then look in the journals for the year or two following date of publication.

The student looking for book reviews in fields other than political science might want to check Richard A. Gray, *A Guide to Book Review Citations; a bibliography of sources* (Columbus: Ohio State Univ. Press, 1968). Gray lists and describes over 500 sources which cite book reviews in various fields.

Chapter 5

United States Government Publications

Government publications cannot be neglected, especially by political science students. *David Estes, a documents librarian*

Government publications have long been the terror of librarians and the despair of almost everyone who has attempted to make use of them. *Alton P. Tisdel, former U.S. Superintendent of Documents*

Both the above statements are exaggerated. Many political science students neglect government publications, manage to survive academically, and lead a normal life. If approached with stout heart and steady mind, government publications need not inspire terror and despair. Both statements, however, contain some truth. Government publications constitute very important source materials in political science and, of all the categories of library materials, they are probably the most difficult for students to use effectively.

I. AVAILABILITY AND TREATMENT IN LIBRARIES

No one, not even the United States government, knows how many United States government publications are issued each year. Depending upon how we define terms, the number would run from a

33

a minimum of about 25,000 to a maximum of perhaps 150,000 per year. Whatever the total is, it is appalling, and a substantial proportion is useful, if not absorbingly interesting, to political scientists.

For better or worse, no library has all government publications which have been issued. In order to ensure widespread distribution of its most important publications, however, the government long ago established a system of depository libraries. There are now over 1,200 depositories across the country, with the majority in college or university libraries. Other libraries, which are not depositories, can purchase government publications, just as they do other materials. There is, of course, vast variation in the proportion of total output which any given library will have. The discussion below centers on bibliographic and reference sources which provide a rather comprehensive approach to government publications. In terms of availability, it probably is skewed toward the upper end of the scale, and the student may need to make some downward adjustments in his own library.

The handling of government publications by libraries resembles guerrilla warfare. Some libraries ignore them, hoping they will go away, which they don't. Others catalog and classify them just as they do other materials, perhaps in the hope that equal treatment will contain and pacify them, which it doesn't. As the tide mounts and more government publications infiltrate the stacks, many larger libraries bring in more troops, set up strategic hamlets in the form of separate "documents departments," and economize by not cataloging their government publications. The solutions are about as numerous as those tried in Vietnam, and they work about as well.

No doubt the reader has drawn the obvious inference. Guerrilla warfare is rough going, and so is this chapter. Consider yourself warned. If you are near graduation anyway, skip it. Others, particularly graduate students, might do well to slog ahead.

II. TYPES OF GOVERNMENT PUBLICATIONS

Modern political science looks with some skepticism on the "separation of powers" provision of the Constitution. For our purposes, however, it will serve as a typology for federal documents:

Executive Publications—These are issued by the various departments, agencies, bureaus, offices, etc., of the Executive Branch. If we include publications of the "independent" agencies and commissions in this category, it constitutes almost 90% of total output.

Congressional Publications—These are the bills, hearings, reports, etc., emanating from Congress and its committees. Today they constitute about 11% of all government publications issued. Because most of them focus on legislation, however, their importance to political scientists is disproportional to their bulk.

Judicial Publications—These consist largely of Supreme Court decisions. The government does not publish decisions of lower federal courts, and judicial publications constitute less than one percent of total output.

All three types must be further sub-divided into "depository" and "non-depository" publications:

Depository Publications—These are printed at the Government Printing Office and are sent automatically to those depository libraries which elect to receive them. Contrary to a widespread impression, however, depository libraries do not receive all government publications, or even all "depository" publications. Some large libraries do take all depository publications, but many libraries select only a small proportion of the total available to them.

Non-Depository Publications—In recent decades more and more federal documents have been printed outside the Government Printing Office, and these are not available to depository libraries. Libraries can acquire some of them by other means, and since 1953 the Readex Microprint Corporation has produced and sold them in microform.

III. A HYPOTHETICAL LIBRARY SITUATION

The hope in the discussion below is to furnish sufficient background for the student to be able to locate and use government publications on his own initiative. The indexes and other reference tools mentioned should be available in most libraries, and familiarity with them will enable him to locate documents "bibliographically." Given the variations in the ways libraries handle government publications, physical location, or actual retrieval of documents, is another matter. Rather than leave the job half done, however, the discussion is cast in terms of a hypothetical library with the following characteristics:

(1) It has an extensive collection of depository publications, and it has non-depository documents in microform.

(2) It does not catalog and classify its documents like regular books, but uses the U.S. Documents Office Classification, shelves its documents in a separate section of the stacks, and depends upon the indexes discussed below for both bibliographic location and physical retrieval.

Students who do not use a library which approximates this model (a familiar quibble in political science) will need to adapt to whatever procedures their libraries have devised for physical location.

IV. INDEXES TO GOVERNMENT PUBLICATIONS

Five basic indexes, covering varying spans of time, provide a reasonably comprehensive listing of federal documents from 1789 to the present:

(1) *United States Government Publications: Monthly Catalog, 1895–* . Washington: Govt. Printing Off., 1895– . Since 1940, this has been the only general list of federal documents. Issued monthly, it lists all publications received by the U.S. Documents Office during the previous month. Contrary to popular belief, it does not list all government documents, but it is comprehensive enough so that the student who learns to use it will, if nothing else, have solved most of his problems in using contemporary government documents.

Documents are listed under the government departments and agencies responsible for their publication, with complete bibliographical information given for each document. Various symbols and numbers appear with each document. The student can ignore most of these, but the following are important for location purposes:

(a) the large black dot, which appears with about half of the publications listed, indicates that the document is a depository publication. These are located through the classification symbol to the lower right of each listing. These symbols will seem strange to the uninitiated, e.g., Y4.Ap6/2:D36/4/964. So far as the student is concerned, they may be considered no more than location devices, serving the same function as the "call numbers" which appear on cards in the card catalog.

(b) Non-depository publications, those without the black dot, are located through the entry number to the left of each publication listed. These numbers are assigned consecutively to documents listed during each year. To locate non-depository documents on Microprint, only the year and entry number are needed.

A subject index, which also contains some author and title entries, appears with each monthly issue of the *Catalog* and is cumulated into an annual index in the December issue. Citations in the index are to the entry numbers in the body of the catalog.

Example of Use—To take only one example of the value of federal publications, suppose you are doing a paper on U.S. policy in Vietnam. You might find a few books through the card catalog, and you would find many articles through the periodical indexes and abstracts discussed in Chapter 3. Most of this would be "secondary" material, however, and for a good term paper you would want some primary sources. The page relating to Vietnam from the annual index to the *Monthly Catalog* for 1967 is reproduced in the accompanying illustration. This shows that altogether there were over 80 different government documents on Vietnam published in 1967. Many of these, such as the document on "slash-burn agriculture among mountain tribes of central Vietnam," may be of no use to you. Two which might be of considerable use are indicated by arrows. The "selected bibliography" has entry number 15805, and the page of the *Monthly Catalog* on which this entry is listed also is reproduced. The publication referred to turns out to be a 16-page bibliography on Vietnam issued by the Foreign Service Institute of the State Department. There is no large black dot, so the bibliography is a non-depository publication available on Microprint, and the only information needed to retrieve it is the year and entry number, i.e., 1967–15805. Entry number 6099 is a hearing held by the Senate Foreign Relations Committee with Edwin O. Reischauer, former U.S. ambassador to Japan. There is a black dot beside the listing, so in this case the classification symbol (Y4.F76/2:As4/5) would be needed to retrieve the document. A quick check of the *Monthly Catalog* for years prior to 1967, and of subsequent issues, would turn up many other documents useful for a paper on this subject.

(2) U.S. Department of Commerce. Clearinghouse for Federal Scientific and Technical Information. *U.S. Government Research & Development Reports*. Washington: Govt. Printing Off., 1946–   . Prior to

15794   6287. Fisheries, certain fisheries off United States coast [and] salmon fisheries, agreements between United States and Japan, effected by exchanges of notes signed Tokyo May 9, 1967; [entered into force May 9, 1967], with Japanese note and agreed minutes. [1967.] [2]+24 p. [Japanese and English.]   * Paper, 15c.
         L.C. card 67–62425

15795   6288. Maritime matters, visit of N.S. Savannah to Hong Kong, agreement between United States and United Kingdom of Great Britain and Northern Ireland. modifying agreement of June 19, 1964, effected by exchange of notes signed London June 12, 1967; [entered into force June 12, 1967]. [1967.] [2]+4 p.   * Paper, 5c.
         L.C. card 67–62339

15796   6289. International trade in cotton textiles, protocol between United States and other governments, extending long-term arrangements of Feb. 9, 1962, done Geneva May 1, 1967; [entered into force Oct. 1, 1967]. [1967.] [2]+4 p. [English and French.]   * Paper, 5c.
         L.C. card 67–62340

15797   6291. Trade in cotton textiles, agreement between United States and Pakistan, effected by exchange of notes signed Washington July 3, 1967; [entered into force July 3, 1967, effective July 1, 1966]. [1967.] [2]+15 p.   * Paper, 10c.
         L.C. card 67–62427

15798   6292. Loan of vessel, agreement between United States and Brazil, effected by exchange of notes signed Washington June 23 and 28, 1967; [entered into force June 28, 1967]. [1967.] [2]+5 p. [English and Portuguese.]   * Paper, 5c.
         L.C. card 67–62341

15799   6303. Maritime matters, liability during private operation of N.S. Savannah, agreement between United States and Republic of China, effected by exchange of notes, dated Taipei Mar. 24, and June 8, 1967; [entered into force June 8, 1967]. [1967.] [2]+6 p. [English and Chinese.]   * Paper, 5c.
         L.C. card 67–62428

15800   6310. Maritime matters, deployment of USS Yellowstone to Malta, agreement between United States and Malta, effected by exchange of notes, signed Valletta July 6 and 25, 1967; [entered into force July 25, 1967]. [1967.] [2]+5 p.   * Paper, 5c.
         L.C. card 67–62429

15801   6312. Atomic energy, cooperation for civil uses, agreement between United States and South Africa, amending agreement of July 8, 1957, as amended, signed Washington July 17, 1967; [entered into force Aug. 17, 1967]. [1967.] [2]+7 p.   * Paper, 10c.
         L.C. card 67–62430

15802   6317. Trade, staging of tariff concessions, agreement between United States and Japan, amending interim agreement of Sept. 6, 1966, effected by exchange of notes. signed Geneva June 30, 1967; [entered into force June 30, 1967]. [1967.] [2]+2 p.   * Paper, 5c.
         L.C. card 67–62431

15803   6318. Trade, staging of tariff concessions, agreement between United States and United Kingdom of Great Britain and Northern Ireland, amending interim agreement of Apr. 5, 1966, effected by exchange of notes signed Geneva June 30, 1967; [entered into force June 30, 1967]. [1967.] [2]+2 p.   * Paper, 5c.
         L.C. card 67–62432

15804   6319. Agricultural commodities, agreement between United States and Viet-Nam, amending agreement of Mar. 13, 1967, effected by exchange of notes signed Saigon July 26, 1967; [entered into force July 26, 1967]. [1967.] [2]+2 p.   * Paper, 5c.
         L.C. card 67–62433

15805 Viet-Nam, selected bibliography. [July 1967.] 16 p. 4°   (Foreign Service Institute, Center for Area and Country Studies.) †   S 1.114/3 : V 67

STATISTICAL REPORTING SERVICE, Agriculture Dept.
Washington, D.C. 20250

15806 Milk production. Aug. 11, 1967. 7 p. il. 4°   (Da 1–1 (8–67) ; Crop Reporting Board.)   [Special in this issue June milk cow numbers.] †
                                                                        A 92.10 : 967/8

TARIFF COMMISSION
Washington, D.C. 20436

15807 Synthetic organic chemicals, United States production and sales of rubber processing chemicals, 1966, preliminary. Aug. 1967. cover title, 9 p. 4° †
                                                                        TC 1.33/2 : R 82

15808 Wilton, Brussels, velvet, and tapestry carpets and rugs, report to the President on investigation no. TEA–I–EX–2 under sec. 351–(d) (3) of Trade

⊕For Sale by Clearinghouse, U.S. Department of
      Commerce, Springfield, Va. 22151
●Sent to Depository Libraries   Page 71

Foreign Relations Committee, Senate
Washington, D.C. 20510

6098 Arms sales and foreign policy, staff study; Jan. 25, 1967. 1967. v+13 p.
(Committee print, 90th Congress, 1st session.) ‡
L.C. card 67–60906   Y 4.F 76/2 : Ar 5/11

6099 Asia, Pacific, and United States, hearing, 90th Congress, 1st session, with
former Ambassador to Japan, Edwin O. Reischauer, Jan. 31, 1967. 1967.
iii+76 p. † ● Item 1039
L.C. card 67–60789   Y 4.F 76/2 : As 4/5

6100 Changing American attitudes toward foreign policy, hearing, 90th Con-
gress, 1st session, with Henry Steele Commager, professor, Amherst
College, Feb. 20, 1967. 1967. iii+59 p. † ● Item 1039
L.C. card 67–60790   Y 4.F 76/2 : F 76/22

6101 Communist world in 1967, hearing, 90th Congress, 1st session, with former
Ambassador to Soviet Union and Yugoslavia George F. Kennan, Jan. 30,
1967. 1967. iii+68 p. † ● Item 1039
L.C. card 67–60791   Y 4.F 76/2 : C 73/5/967

6102 Conflicts between United States capabilities and foreign commitments,
hearing, 90th Congress, 1st session, with James M. Gavin, on Feb. 21,
1967. 1967. iii+44 p. † ● Item 1039
L.C. card 67–60792   Y 4.F 76/2 : F 76/21

6103 Consular convention with Soviet Union, hearings, 90th Congress, 1st session, on Executive D, 88th Congress, 2d session, Jan. 23–Feb. 17, 1967.
1967. iv+374 p. il. † ● Item 1039   Y 4.F 76/2 : So 8/4

6104 East of the Elbe, report by Senator Joseph S. Clark on study mission to
Warsaw, Moscow, Belgrade, and Prague; Jan. 23, 1967. 1967. v+14 p.
(Committee print, 90th Congress, 1st session.) ‡
L.C. card 67–60908   Y 4.F 76/2 : E 1

6105 Harrison E. Salisbury's trip to North Vietnam, hearing, 90th Congress, 1st
session, with Harrison E. Salisbury, assistant managing editor of New
York times, Feb. 2, 1967. 1967. iii+151 p. † ● Item 1039
L.C. card 67–60795   Y 4.F 76/2 : V 67/10

6106 Legislation on foreign relations, with explanatory notes: Jan. 1967. 1967.
xi+876 p. (Foreign Relations Committee, Senate, Foreign Affairs Committee, House, joint committee print, 90th Congress, 1st session.) [Pre-
pared by officials in various departments and agencies of executive
branch in collaboration with staffs of Committee on Foreign Relations
and Foreign Affairs. Contains text of laws as amended through 2d
session of 89th Congress. Edge index and how to use on p. 4 of cover.] ‡
L.C. card 57–60766   Y 4.F 76/2 : L 52/967

6107 Nomination of William M. Roth, to be Special Representative for Trade
Negotiations, hearing, 90th Congress, 1st session, Feb. 27, 1967. 1967.
iii+50 p. † ● Item 1039   Y 4.F 76/2 : R 74

Government Operations Committee, Senate
Washington, D.C. 20510

6108 Atlantic alliance, unfinished business, study submitted by Subcommittee on
National Security and International Operations, pursuant to S. Res. 54,
90th Congress. 1967. v+15 p. (Committee print, 90th Congress, 1st
session.) ‡ ● Item 1037
L.C. card 67–60880   Y 4.G 74/6 : At 6/3/967

6109 Disposal of United States military installations and supplies in France,
report by Senator Ernest Gruening, chairman, Subcommittee on Foreign
Aid Expenditures, Jan. 30, 1967. 1967. vi+47 p. il. (Committee print,
90th Congress, 1st session.) ‡
L.C. card 67–60907   Y 4.G 74/6 : F 84

World War II, practically all government research was conducted by scientists employed by the government. Since World War II, however, the federal government has increasingly secured its research needs via contracts with private individuals and research organizations. One of the products of this research is publication, and thousands of contract research reports now appear each year. Few of them are listed in the *Monthly Catalog;* most relate to scientific and technical disciplines and are of little interest to the political scientist. In recent years, however, as the government has provided more research support for the social sciences, an increasing number of relevant research reports has appeared. Those which are not classified for security reasons are listed and abstracted in *U.S. Government Research & Development Reports,* now published semi-monthly. Reports are arranged by twenty-one broad subject fields; Field 5 covers "Behavioral and Social Sciences" and has a section on "History, Law, and Political Science." A companion publication, *U.S. Government Research & Development Reports Index,* provides subject and author indexes to publications listed. These reports are not distributed to depository libraries, though large libraries may purchase the most important ones, and they can be bought at nominal cost by individuals. This bibliography will not be a major source for most students, but those who are working on subjects in which the government has a direct interest, such as military or foreign policy or public administration, might find it well worth checking.

(3) *Catalog of the Public Documents of Congress and of All Departments of the Government of the United States for the Period March 4, 1893–December 31, 1940.* Washington: Govt. Printing Off., 1896–1945. Generally referred to as the "Documents Catalog." Publications are listed by subject, governmental and personal author, and by title. It is, roughly, a card catalog of government publications in book form. Though listing many publications, particularly non-depository items, not listed in the *Monthly Catalog* for these years, it is largely a duplication of the *Monthly Catalog,* differing in format and extensiveness of indexing. Classification symbols are not given, thus it is not possible to go directly from the "Documents Catalog" to the shelf to retrieve publications. The student who must do extensive searching for documents of the 1893–1940 period should use this as a supplement to the *Monthly Catalog*; most students can safely ignore it.

(4) Ames, John G. *Comprehensive Index to the Publications of the United States Government, 1881–1893.* Washington: Govt. Printing

Off., 1905. The only general listing for these years. During this period relatively few Executive publications were issued, thus Ames is chiefly a listing of Congressional documents. Format is three columns per page, with key arrangement by subject in the second column. Third column gives congress, session, volume of the series, and number for Congressional publications.

(5) Poore, Benjamin P. *A Descriptive Catalogue of the Government Publications of the United States, September 5, 1774–March 4, 1881.* Washington: Govt. Printing Off., 1885. Arrangement is chronological by date of publication, with a subject index. Chiefly Congressional publications. The index is difficult to use, and Southerners will find it insulting. (The War Between the States is indexed as "Rebellion.") Despite its shortcomings, Poore is the only listing for this early period.

V. LEGISLATIVE TRACING

The indexes above list Congressional as well as Executive publications. Most Congressional publications, however, are not classified by the Documents Office system and must be located by different methods. The student who is interested only in material on a particular subject will not care whether it appears as an Executive or Congressional publication, and for him the location process will be relatively simple. The student who is focusing on a particular piece of legislation, however, must become involved in the intricacies of "legislative tracing." At some point in their career, either as an exercise in a basic course on American Government and Politics or later, in a more serious and substantive vein, most students will have to get their hands dirty by following a bill through the legislative process.

Here we will attempt to do two things at once: discuss the five basic publications emanating from the legislative process and trace a particular piece of legislation—the Appalachian Development Act—through Congress in order to show how to retrieve the publications involved.

The essential key to legislative tracing is a status table, or history of legislation, which presents the skeletal information necessary to follow legislation through the Congressional maze. Status tables, which list bills and indicate action taken on them, are available in various publications and in various formats. Two status tables, both on the Appalachian Development Act, are reproduced on the following pages. The first is from the privately published *Congressional Index* (Chicago: Commerce Clearing House, 1937/38–   ). Since this service is rather expensive and may not be available in many libraries, a similar table from the *Congressional Record* (Washington: Govt. Printing Off., 1873–   ), which should be available in practically all college or university libraries, also is reproduced. Reference will be made to both tables in the discussion below, and, as we will see, considerable digging is required to flesh out their skeletons with documentation.

(1) Bills and Resolutions—The first publication arising from the legislative process is a bill or resolution. These are numbered consecutively as introduced, in the House or Senate, through each Congress, e.g., H.R. 9187 or S. 2431, 89th Congress. In libraries which have them, bills usually are filed by Congress and bill number. The *Digest of Public General Bills with Index* (Washington: Govt. Printing Off., 1936–   ) gives a good summary of the content and purpose of each bill. Both the *Digest* and the *Congressional Index* have subject indexes to all bills introduced, through which one can find the number of a bill on a particular subject. In our example, one of these indexes was used to find that the Appalachian Development Act was S. 3 of the 89th Congress. Once the bill number is ascertained, we can begin the tracing process through a status table.

Currently over 20,000 bills are introduced in the House of Representatives during each Congress and over 4,000 in the Senate. After introduction, they are referred to one of the standing committees of the House or Senate, and nine out of ten bills die right there. If a bill is important or has enough pressure behind it, however, it will move on to the second stage in the legislative process:

(2) Hearings—These are the printed records of hearings held by committees on pending legislation or as part of Congressional investigations. They are probably the most important publications originating with Congress, frequently containing primary data not available in any other sources but, unfortunately, some hearings, usually those in executive session, are never published. Note, that the status table from the *Congressional Record* does not even mention a hearing on the Appalachian Development Bill. This is because hear-

LEGISLATIVE HISTORY OF SENATE BILLS APPROVED OR VETOED DURING FIRST SESSION

➡➡ Arrangement by Bill numbers—For Digests see same numbers in "Senate Bills" division.

3

Hearing in S. 1/19/65
S. hearing available 2/9/65
Reptd., with amend., S. Rept. 13 ... 1/27/65
Amended on S. Floor [Voice] 2/1/65
Passed S., with amend. [Roll-call] .. 2/1/65
To H. Public Works 2/2/65
Hearing in H. 2/3/65
H. hearing available 3/17/65
Reptd., no amend., H. Rept. 51 ..... 2/17/65
Recommittal motion rejected by H.
[Roll-call] 3/3/65
Passed H., without amend. [Roll-call]
.... 3/3/65
Approved [Public Law 89-4].......... 3/9/65

4

Hearing in S. 1/18/65
S. hearing available 2/9/65
Reptd., with amend., S. Rept. 10 ... 1/27/65
Amended on S. Floor [Roll-call] ... 1/28/65
Passed S., with amend. [Roll-call] .....
.... 1/28/65
To H. Public Works 2/1/65
Hearing in H. 2/18/65
H. hearing available 4/5/65
Reptd., with amend., H. Rept. 215 ......
.... 3/31/65
Amended on H. Floor [Voice]....... 4/28/65
Passed H., with amend. [Roll-call] .....
.... 4/28/65
S. appoints conferees 7/28/65
H. appoints conferees 7/29/65
Conf. Rept. submitted to H., H. Rept.
1022 .... 9/17/65
Conf. Rept. agreed to by H. [Roll-call]
.... 9/21/65
Conf. Rept. agreed to by S. 9/21/65
Approved [Public Law 89-234]...... 10/2/65

7

Hearing in S. 4/1/65
S. hearing available 4/28/65
Reptd., with amend., S. Rept. 507 .. 7/22/65
Passed S., as reptd. [Voice].......... 7/23/65
To H. Agriculture 7/26/65
H. Com. discharged 9/7/65

Amended on H. Floor [Voice] 9/7/65
Passed H., with amend., in lieu of
H. 10330 [Voice] 9/7/65
H. amend. agreed to by S. 9/14/65
Approved [Public Law 89-207]...... 9/28/65

20

Hearing in S. 3/17/65
S. hearing available 6/8/65
Reptd., with amend., S. Rept. 331 ....
.... 6/15/65
Passed S., as reptd. [Voice].......... 6/17/65
To H. Interior and Insular Affairs
.... 6/21/65
Hearing in H. 7/22/65
H. hearing available 9/29/65
H. Com. discharged 9/7/65
Amended on H. Floor [Voice] 9/7/65
Passed H., with amend., in lieu of
H. 2071 [Voice] 9/7/65
H. amend. agreed to by S. 9/15/65
Approved [Public Law 89-195]...... 9/21/65

21

Hearing in S. 2/5/65
S. hearing available 3/17/65
Hearing in S. 2/8/65
Reptd., with amend., S. Rept. 68 ... 2/24/65
Passed S., as reptd. [Voice].......... 2/25/65
To H. Interior and Insular Affairs ......
.... 3/1/65
H. Com. discharged 3/31/65
Amended on H. Floor [Voice] 3/31/65
Passed H., with amend., in lieu of
H. 1111 [Voice] 3/31/65
S. appoints conferees 4/9/65
H. appoints conferees 4/13/65
Conf. Rept. submitted to H., H. Rept.
603 .... 7/8/65
Conf. Rept. agreed to by H. 7/13/65
Conf. Rept. agreed to by S. 7/14/65
Approved [Public Law 89-80]........ 7/22/65

24

Hearing in S. 5/18/65
Reptd., no amend., S. Rept. 319 .... 6/14/65
Passed S., without amend. [Voice] ......
.... 6/16/65

Congressional Index—1965-1966

Status Table from *Congressional Index*

HISTORY OF BILLS AND RESOLUTIONS

SENATE BILLS

S. 1—To provide a hospital insurance program for the aged under security, to amend the Federal Old-Age, Survivors, and Disability Insurance System to increase benefits, improve the actuarial status of the Disability Insurance Trust Fund, and extend coverage, to amend the Social Security Act to provide additional Federal financial participation in the Federal-State public assistance programs, and for other purposes.
Mr. Anderson, Mr. Gore, Mr. Javits, Mc-Namara, Mr. Bartlett, Mr. Bayh, Mr. Bible, Mr. Brewster, Mr. Burdick, Mr. Case, Mr. Church, Mr. Clark, Mr. Dodd, Mr. Douglas, Mr. Gruening, Mr. Hartke, Mr. Inouye, Mr. Jackson, Mr. Kennedy of Massachusetts, Mr. Kennedy of New York, Mr. Kuchel, Mr. Long of Missouri, Mr. Mansfield, Mr. McCarthy, Mr. McGee, Mr. McGovern, Mr. McIntyre, Mr. Metcalf, Mr. Mondale, Mr. Monroney, Mr. Montoya, Mr. Morse, Mr. Moss, Mr. Muskie, Mrs. Neuberger, Mr. Pastore, Mr. Pell, Mr. Proxmire, Mr. Randolph, Mr. Ribicoff, Mr. Tydings, Mr. Williams of New Jersey, Mr. Yarborough, and Mr. Young or Ohio; Committee on Finance, 166, 537.

S. 2—To amend the Legislative Reorganization Act of 1946 to provide for more effective evalution of the fiscal requirements of the executive agencies of the Government of the United States.
Mr. McClellan, Mr. Allott, Mr. Anderson, Mr. Bartlett, Mr. Bayh, Mr. Bennett, Mr. Bible, Mr. Boggs, Mr. Brewster, Mr. Burdick, Mr. Byrd of Virginia, Mr. Cannon, Mr. Carlson, Mr. Case, Mr. Cooper, Mr. Curtis, Mr. Dirksen, Mr. Dodd, Mr. Dominick, Mr. Eastland, Mr. Ervin, Mr. Fannin, Mr. Fong, Mr. Fulbright, Mr. Gruening, Mr. Harris, Mr. Hartke, Mr. Hickenlooper, Mr. Holland, Mr. Hruska, Mr. Inouye, Mr. Jackson, Mr. Javits, Mr. Johnston, Mr. Jordan of North Carolina, Mr. Jordan of Idaho, Mr. Kennedy of New York, Mr. Kuchel, Mr. Lausche, Mr. Magnuson, Mr. McGee, Mr. McGovern, Mr. Miller, Mr. Mondale, Mr. Monroney, Mr. Montoya, Mr. Morse, Mr. Morton, Mr. Moss, Mr. Mundt, Mr. Murphy, Mr. Muskie, Mr. Nelson, Mrs. Neuberger, Mr. Pastore, Mr. Pearson, Mr. Pell, Mr. Prouty, Mr. Proxmire, Mr. Randolph, Mr. Ribicoff, Mr. Saltonstall, Mr. Scott, Mr. Simpson, Mr. Smathers, Mr. Sparkman, Mr. Stennis, Mr. Symington, Mr. Talmadge, Mr. Thurmond, Mr. Tower, Mr. Tydings, Mr. Williams of New Jersey, Mr. Williams of Delaware, Mr. Yarborough, Mr. Young of North Dakota, and Mr. Young of Ohio; Committee on Government Operations, 166, 1039.—Reported (S. Rept. 6), 1229.—Passed Senate, 1359.—Referred to House Committee on Rules, 1456.

S. 3—To provide public works and economic development programs and the planning and cordination needed to assist in the development of the Appalachian region.
Mr. Randolph, Mr. Cooper, Mr. Anderson, Mr. Bartlett, Mr. Bass, Mr. Bayh, Mr. Brewster, Mr. Burdick, Mr. Byrd of West

S. 3—Continued
Virginia, Mr. Clark, Mr. Dodd, Mr. Douglas, Mr. Gore, Mr. Gruening, Mr. Hart, Mr. Hartke, Mr. Inouye, Mr. Johnston, Mr. Kennedy of Massachusetts, Mr. Magnuson, Mr. McCarthy, Mr. McGovern, Mr. McNamara, Mr. Metcalf, Mr. Mondale, Mr. Morse, Mr. Morton, Mr. Moss, Mr. Nelson, Mrs. Neuberger, Mr. Pell, Mr. Ribicoff, Mr. Scott, Mr. Tydings, Mr. Williams of New Jersey, Mr. Yarborough, and Mr. Young of Ohio; Committee on Public Works, 166, 912.—Reported with amendment (S. Rept. 13), 1460.—Debated, 1543, 1550, 1575, 1609, 1671, 1688, 1690, 1691, 1706.—Amended and passed Senate, 1715.—Referred to House Committee on Public Works, 1858.—Reported (H. Rept. 51), 2946.—Made special order (H. Res. 249), 3844.—Debated, 3847, 3915, 3997.—Passed House, 4030.—Examined and signed, 4077, 4240.—Presented to the President, 4118.—Approved [Public Law 89-4], 4578.

S. 4—To amend the Federal Water Pollution Control Act, as amended, to establish the Federal Water Pollution Control Administration, to provide grants for research and development, to increase grants for construction of municipal sewage treatment works, to authorize the establishment of standards of water quality to aid in preventing, controlling, and abating pollution of interstate waters, and for other purposes.
Mr. Muskie, Mr. Bartlett, Mr. Bayh, Mr. Boggs, Mr. Brewster, Mr. Clark, Mr. Douglas, Mr Fong, Mr. Gruening, Mr. Hart, Mr. Inouye, Mr. Kennedy of Massachusetts, Mr. Long of Missouri, Mr. Magnuson, Mr. McCarthy, Mr. McGee, Mr. Metcalf, Mr. Miller, Mr. Moss, Mr. Nelson, Mrs. Neuberger, Mr. Pearson, Mr. Pell, Mr. Randolph, Mr. Ribicoff, Mr. Tydings, Mr. Williams of New Jersey, and Mr. Young of Ohio; Committee on Public Works, 166.—Reported with amendments (S. Rept. 10), 1350.—Debated, 1370, 1501, 1503, 1508, 1511, 1524, 1542, 1543.—Amended and passed Senate, 1545.—Referred to House Committee on Public Works, 1654.—Reported with amendment (H. Rept. 215), 6452.—Made special order (H. Res. 339), 8652.—Debated, amended, and passed House, 8654.—Title amended, 8690.—Senate disagrees to House amendments and asks for a conference. 18535.—Conferees appointed, 18537.—House insists on its amendments and agrees to a conference, 18691.—Conferees appointed, 18691.—Conference report (H. Rept. 1022) submitted in House and agreed to, 24583.—Conference report submitted in Senate and agreed to, 24560.—Examined and signed, 24718, 24785.—Presented to the President, 24724.—Approved [Public Law 89-234], 25990.

S. 5—To provide assistance for students in higher education by establishing programs for student grants, loan insurance, and work-study.
Mr. Hartke, Mr. Bartlett, Mr. Bayh, Mr. Burdick, Mr. Cannon, Mr. Church, Mr.

S. 5—Continued
Clark, Mr. Douglas, Mr. Gruening, Mr. Hart, Mr. Inouye, Mr. Jordan of North Carolina, Mr. Kennedy of Massachusetts, Mr. Long of Missouri, Mr. McCarthy, Mr. McGee, Mr. McGovern, Mr. McIntyre, Mr. Montoya, Mr. Moss, Mr. Muskie, Mr. Pell, Mr. Randolph, Mr. Tydings, Mr. Yarborough, and Mr. Young of North Dakota; Committee on Labor and Public Welfare, 166, 912, 1485.

S. 6—To provide for the establishment and administration of the Allegheny Parkway in the States of West Virginia and Kentucky and Maryland, and for other purposes.
Mr. Byrd of West Virginia, Mr. Randolph, Mr. Cooper, Mr. Brewster, Mr. Morton, and Mr. Tydings; Committee on Interior and Insular Affairs, 166.

S. 7—To provide for the establishment of the Spruce Knob-Seneca Rocks National Recreation Area, in the State of West Virginia, and for other purposes.
Mr. Byrd of West Virginia and Mr. Randolph; Committee on Agriculture and Forestry; 166.—Reported with amendments (S. Rept. 507), 17877.—Amended and passed Senate, 18035.—Referred to House Committee on Agriculture, 18165.—Committee discharged, passed House (in lieu of H.R. 10330), 22955.—Proceedings vacated, amended and passed House, 23009.—Senate concurs in House amendment, 23792.—Examined and signed, 23868, 24017.—Presented to the President, 24152.—Approved [Public Law 89-207], 25535.

S. 8—To provide for a program of Federal assistance for the construction of public elementary and secondary schools.
Mr. McNamara; Committee on Labor and Public Welfare, 166.

S. 9—To provide readjustment assistance to veterans who serve in the Armed Forces during the induction period.
Mr. Yarborough, Mr. Bartlett, Mr. Bayh, Mr. Bible, Mr. Boggs, Mr. Burdick, Mr. Byrd of West Virginia, Mr. Cannon, Mr. Clark, Mr. Dodd, Mr. Douglas, Mr. Eastland, Mr. Fong, Mr. Fulbright, Mr. Gruening, Mr. Hart, Mr. Hartke, Mr. Hill, Mr. Inouye, Mr. Johnston, Mr. Long of Missouri, Mr. McCarthy, Mr. McGee, Mr. McGovern, Mr. Metcalf, Mr. Mondale, Mr. Montoya, Mr. Morse, Mr. Moss, Mr. Nelson, Mrs. Neuberger, Mr. Pastore, Mr. Pell, Mr. Randolph, Mrs. Smith, Mr. Sparkman, Mr. Tydings, Mr. Williams of New Jersey, and Mr. Young of Ohio; Committee on Labor and Public Welfare, 167, 745, 3556.—Reported with amendments (S. Rept. 269), 12113.—Debated, 16962, 17127, 17154, 17297, 17301, 17303, 17308, 17316, 17325.—Amended and passed Senate, 17348.—Referred to House Committee on Veterans' Affairs, 17575.

S. 10—To amend the antitrust laws to prohibit certain activities of labor organizations in restraint of trade, and for other purposes.
Mr. McClellan, Mr. Byrd of Virginia, Mr. Bennett, Mr. Eastland, Mr. Robertson,

1199

Status Table from *Congressional Record*

ings take place off the floor of Congress and are not considered official actions of Congress as a body. The status table from the *Congressional Index* indicates that a hearing was held on S. 3 in the Senate on January 19, 1965, and that this hearing became "available," i.e., was published, on February 9th.

If we turn to the annual index to the *Monthly Catalog* for 1965, under the subject heading "Appalachian region" we find reference to a hearing with the entry number 4620. Turning to the body of the *Catalog* under this entry number, we find the hearing referred to in the status table, a 208-page publication of the Senate Public Works Committee on the "Appalachian Regional Development Act of 1965." There is a black dot, meaning that the publication is a depository item, thus we can retrieve it by the classification symbol, Y4.P96/10:Ap4/965.

(3) Reports—After holding hearings the committee normally will write a report on the bill stating its reasons for approving it. If it disapproves, usually no report will be written, and the committee will let the bill expire silently. If the committee is divided there may be separate majority and minority reports. Reports are numbered consecutively for House and Senate through a Congress, but report numbers will bear no relation to bill numbers. In our example, both status tables show that the Senate committee made a report, S. Rept. 13, on this bill.

Libraries receive reports initially in separate, unbound form as they are printed, and they can be located simply by Congress and report number, in this case Senate Report 13, 89th Congress. After a year or so, however, reports also are distributed in a series of bound volumes known as the *Serial Set* or *Congressional Edition,* and most libraries will discard the initial unbound copies. To retrieve committee reports more than a year or two old, it is necessary to discover which bound volume of the *Serial Set* (there are over 12,000 volumes) contains the report wanted. So long as you have the Congress and report number, this can be done easily by using the following reference tools for the periods indicated: *Checklist of United States Public Documents* (1789–1909), *Document Index* (1895–1933), and *Numerical Lists and Schedule of Volumes* (1933–   ).

(4) Floor Debate—After being reported out of committee, a bill is placed on a legislative "calendar" and eventually, in most cases, will be called up for debate. The current official record of the de-

bates in Congress is the *Congressional Record,* published since 1873. A daily edition of the *Record* is available within one or two days after debate has taken place. This is later superseded by a bound edition, running to about 15 large volumes for each session of Congress. Both editions have an index consisting of two sections: (a) "Index to the Proceedings" in which indexing is very complete under the names of Congressmen (there are eight close-print pages in the index for the second session of the 88th Congress under "Morse, Wayne, a Senator from Oregon"), but subject indexing is weak; (b) "History of Bills and Resolutions" which contains citations, by bill number, to all debate and other action on bills which reach the floor of either house of Congress. This is the section from which the second status table is taken. Records of debate prior to 1873 appear in: *Annals of Congress* (1789–1824), *Register of Debates* (1824–1837), *Congressional Globe* (1822–1873).

In the status table from the *Congressional Index,* you will note that S. 3 was amended on the Senate floor by voice vote on February 1, 1965, and passed the Senate by roll call vote the same day. The status table from the *Congressional Record* refers directly to the pages on which the debate may be found.

After passage by the Senate, both status tables indicate that the Appalachian Development Act was referred to the House Committee on Public Works. In the House it had to go through the same steps— hearing, report, floor debate—and the publications arising from passage through the House may be located in exactly the same manner as outlined above for the Senate. Finally, we end up with the fifth publication necessary for legislative tracing:

(5) Laws—These are numbered consecutively as passed by Congress and signed by the President. In this case, as shown in the status tables, S. 3 became Public Law number 4 of the 89th Congress. The first printing of laws is in separate "slip law" form, and they can be located simply by Congress and law number. Slips laws are superseded by the *Statutes at Large,* each volume (there are now over 70) containing the text of all laws passed by each session of a Congress. The *United States Code* provides a subject codification of all laws, or sections or laws, presently in force.

Thus we complete a very simple and easy job of legislative tracing. No irony is intended. The Appalachian Development Act was an "Administration bill" with much steam behind it, and it went through

Congress in two months, like the proverbial dose. Many bills run into delays and obstructions which considerably complicate the job of legislative tracing. If you have to do such a job, and have any choice in the matter, do a little checking first and pick carefully. Any bill backed jointly by the President and the opposition leadership will do very nicely.

The student who needs a crutch in using Congressional publications, particularly in legislative tracing, will find strong support in the *Congressional Quarterly Weekly Report* (Washington: Congressional Quarterly, Inc., 1943–   ) and the *Congressional Quarterly Almanac* (Washington: Congressional Quarterly, Inc., 1945–   ). These reference tools analyze action in Congress, give summaries of hearings, reports, and debate, plus records of all votes taken. They are not discussed in detail here, since the student no doubt has encountered them in his course work and may, in fact, have discovered that they can be used as short-cuts in legislative tracing or as substitutes for Congressional publications themselves.

VI. JUDICIAL PUBLICATIONS

Supreme Court decisions are printed in separate form and made available shortly after they are handed down. Decisions are later brought together in bound form in a series known as *United States Reports*. Beyond this, the government publishes very few judicial documents. To obtain decisions of district and circuit courts, or briefs and oral arguments before the Supreme Court, it is necessary to consult privately-published "law services." Location and use of judicial materials have been covered well in other guides, and rather than clutter up this one the reader who needs some help in this area is referred to Miles O. Price and Harry Bitner's *Effective Legal Research* (Boston: Little, Brown, 1962).

VII. NOTE ON THE VALUE OF FEDERAL PUBLICATIONS

The utility of federal documents will vary with the sub-field of political science in which a student is working. For those in U.S. government and politics, American foreign policy, or area studies, they will be indispensable. The student of public administration below the federal level, or of state and local government, might find them somewhat less useful, though even here, to take only one example, the publications of the U.S. Advisory Committee on Intergovernmental Relations would be relevant. About the only area of political science where federal documents might be of little value is political philosophy, but even here the *Congressional Record* or the texts of Presidential speeches and news conferences would provide raw material for a content analysis sufficient to short-circuit any computer. With most research problems in political science, it would be advisable to take at least a quick look at the indexes described above.

Additional Information—The student who needs more details on federal publications might want to consult:

(1) Schmeckebier, Laurence F. and Roy B. Eastin. *Government Publications and Their Use.* rev. ed. Washington: Brookings Inst., 1961.

(2) Boyd, Anne M. and Rae E. Rips. *United States Government Publications.* 3rd ed. New York: H. W. Wilson, 1949.

Chapter 6

Publications of the United Nations and Other International Organizations

In many cases publications of the United Nations and other international organizations will be of equal or greater value to the political science student than U.S. government publications. Someone studying the Congo crisis, the India-Pakistan border dispute, or the Arab-Israeli flareups would find UN publications indispensable as primary source material. In areas where the United Nations has no direct peace-keeping responsibility, there will be much information in UN publications not available in any other sources. On such subjects as economic and political development, disarmament, and methodological developments in the social sciences, UN, Unesco, and other international agency publications will be useful.

I. AVAILABILITY AND TREATMENT IN LIBRARIES

Though its output of publications is far less mountainous than that of the federal government, the United Nations consumes its share of print. Again depending upon how we define terms, a minimum of about 6,000 and a maximum of around 10,000 publications and documents pour forth from the UN headquarters each year. There is a network of depository libraries through which these materials are made available to the public, but—in contrast to the 800-plus depositories for United States publications—there are only 33 United Nations depository libraries in this country. (If this seems too few, the Russians have only three.) Many other American libraries, however, purchase the more important UN publications. The Readex Microprint Corporation also produces a Microprint edition of UN publications which is bought by a number of American libraries. A "List of Libraries and Information Centers Receiving United Nations Material" appears annually as Part 2 of *United Nations Documents Index: Cumulative Index,* which is described below.

Library handling of United Nations publications generally follows the guerrilla warfare pattern outlined for U.S. publications in the last chapter. Because the total output is less, however, and for other reasons, apparently more libraries classify and catalog their UN publications just as they do other materials. In these libraries, the card catalog will provide at least some bibliographic and physical approaches to UN documents. Knowledge of the indexes and bibliographies described below, however, still will be essential to full exploitation of UN publications. In libraries which do not catalog United Nations documents, these indexes and bibliographies may be the only approaches available.

One other element enters into the use of UN publications which is not present—or present to a lesser degree—with U.S. government publications. UN publications are designed primarily to facilitate the work of the UN itself; public use is a secondary factor, and this is reflected in the pattern of document publication and issue. This introduces certain complications which make it necessary to know at least in general terms the structure of the United Nations and its subdivisions. The student who is unfamiliar with this structure would do well, before attempting to use UN publications, to glance through any good textbook on the UN or to consult *Everyman's United Nations* (New York: United Nations, Dept. of Public Information. 8th ed., 1968) a handbook issued by the UN, which contains a concise account of its operation and structure.

As in Chapter 5, in the discussion here we assume a hypothetical library with a large UN collection which it does not catalog, and in which the indexes described below are used for bibliographic access and physical retrieval.

II. TYPES OF UNITED NATIONS PUBLICATIONS

At the risk of some distortion, we can place United Nations materials in two broad categories:

(1) Mimeographed Documents—Most items emanating from the UN appear originally in mimeographed form. This is done to allow fast production and distribution to delegates, committees, etc., who need the materials in their deliberations. Some of these mimeographed documents are later printed, but many remain only in mimeographed form. Generally, only depository libraries, and a few large libraries with sufficient funds to purchase them, will have all mimeographed documents.

(2) Printed Publications—The category is self-explanatory, but for our purposes must be further subdivided into:

(a) Official Records—These are the records of the proceedings of the five main organs of the United Nations: the General Assembly, Security Council, Economic and Social Council, Trusteeship Council, and Disarmament Commission. They consist primarily of transcripts of meetings and important documents used in the work of these organs and can be considered the UN equivalents of the U.S. *Congressional Record*. Many documents issued originally in mimeographed form will be "republished" in the *Official Records* of these organs.

(b) "Sales Number" Publications—These are items for which some public demand is expected and which are printed and offered for sale to the general public and to libraries.

III. CLASSIFICATION SYSTEM

All mimeographed documents and most printed publications are classified by the United Nations under a system basically similar to that used for U.S. government publications, with the primary classification by issuing agency rather than by subject. Thus the symbol A/AC.105/INF.39 stands for the 39th document in the information series (INF) of the Committee on the Peaceful Uses of Outer Space

(AC.105) of the General Assembly (A). These are called "documents series symbols," but in most cases students need not worry about what the hieroglyphics mean. In libraries which classify their materials by the United Nations system, these symbols serve the same function as "call numbers" in the card catalog.

In the indexes described below, many "sales number" publications will not have symbols like the one above. Instead, you may see such things as this: 63.XIV.2. This is the "sales number" for a publication entitled *Study of Discrimination in the Matter of Political Rights,* issued by the Sub-Commission on Prevention of Discrimination and Protection of Minorities of the Commission on Human Rights of the Economic and Social Council of the United Nations. (The UN, too, has its bureaucracy.) There is so much variety in the ways libraries handle and shelve "sales number" publications that an attempt to explain would only confuse. If the student gets this far and locates a publication "bibliographically," he has done well and can turn to the library staff for physical location.

IV. INDEXES TO UNITED NATIONS DOCUMENTS AND PUBLICATIONS

(1) The most important source for locating UN materials is the *United Nations Documents Index* (New York: United Nations Library. Documents Index Unit, 1950–   ) issued monthly and cumulated yearly. Each issue will contain a puzzling array of sections, numbers, abbreviations, etc. Most of these can be ignored, but the following are important:

(a) The "Checklist of Documents and Publications"—Each month this lists both mimeographed documents and printed publications under the agency of the UN responsible for their publication. The arrangement is hierarchical, that is, under the General Assembly those items which relate to the work of the Assembly as a whole (called "plenary" documents) will be listed first, followed by the documents and publications of the various committees, subcommittees, etc., of the General Assembly. Documents series symbols and/or sales numbers will be listed for each item.

(b) The "Subject Index"—This indexes the documents and publications listed in the Checklist section. References are to documents series symbols or sales numbers rather than to page numbers.

Though primarily a subject index, there also are entries under the titles of publications and by UN agencies.

Both the Checklist and Subject Index sections of the *United Nations Documents Index* are cumulated into a single annual volume at the end of each year. Prior to 1963, the format of the index was different from that described above, but students should be able to adjust to it without great difficulty.

An example of how to use the *United Nations Documents Index* may be followed in the accompanying illustrations. The first is a reproduction of one page from the subject index to the June, 1968, issue of the *UNDI*. Suppose you wanted to read the Secretary General's report relating to Southern Rhodesia's unilateral declaration of independence. The documents series symbol given is S/ 7781/Add.5, which is addition number 5 to Security Council document number 7781. The second illustration shows the page from the Checklist section of the same issue on which this document is listed. It is a 100-page report by Secretary-General U Thant in pursuance of an earlier resolution of the Security Council on Southern Rhodesia. The only information needed to retrieve it is the documents series symbol, S/7781/Add.5. Frequently mimeographed documents such as this one will be "republished," that is, printed as part of the *Official Records* of the main organ, for which see below.

(2) Indexes to Proceedings—These are indexes to the debates and proceedings of the main organs. A separate index is issued for each session of the General Assembly, Security Council, Economic and Social Council, and Trusteeship Council. There is a "Subject Index" section which provides a subject approach to the debates and other proceedings of each organ and its committees. An "Index to Speeches" section allows one to find out what the representatives from each member country in the UN had to say on different subjects. Prior to 1953, the *Indexes to Proceedings* were issued under the title, *Disposition of Agenda Items*.

A page from the "Index to Speeches" for the 21st Session of the General Assembly is reproduced on a following page. Suppose you wanted to read what the Soviet representatives had to say about the Vietnam situation. The reference reads: "Plen: 1413, 1461, 1499," which means Plenary Record numbers 1413, 1461, and 1499 of the General Assembly. A separate printed record of proceedings is pro-

General Assembly
Security Council

Meeting Records

A/CONF. 39/C. 1/SR. 45-77. Summary records.

*SR. 45	45th meeting	30 Apr 1968
*SR. 46	46th meeting	30 Apr 1968
*SR. 47	47th meeting	2 May 1968
*SR. 48	48th meeting	2 May 1968
*SR. 49	49th meeting	2 May 1968
*SR. 50	50th meeting	3 May 1968
*SR. 51	51st meeting	3 May 1968
*SR. 52	52nd meeting	4 May 1968
*SR. 53	53rd meeting	6 May 1968
*SR. 54	54th meeting	6 May 1968
*SR. 55	55th meeting	7 May 1968
*SR. 56	56th meeting	7 May 1968
*SR. 57	57th meeting	7 May 1968
*SR. 58	58th meeting	8 May 1968
*SR. 59	59th meeting	8 May 1968
*SR. 60	60th meeting	9 May 1968
*SR. 61	61st meeting	9 May 1968

Meeting Records (continued)

A/CONF. 39/C. 1/SR. 45-77. Summary records (continued).

*SR. 62	62nd meeting	9 May 1968
*SR. 63	63rd meeting	10 May 1968
*SR. 64	64th meeting	10 May 1968
*SR. 65	65th meeting	11 May 1968
*SR. 66	66th meeting	13 May 1968
*SR. 67	67th meeting	13 May 1968
*SR. 68	68th meeting	14 May 1968
*SR. 69	69th meeting	14 May 1968
*SR. 70	70th meeting	14 May 1968
*SR. 71	71st meeting	15 May 1968
*SR. 72	72nd meeting	15 May 1968
*SR. 73	73rd meeting	16 May 1968
*SR. 74	74th meeting	16 May 1968
*SR. 75	75th meeting	17 May 1968
*SR. 76	76th meeting	17 May 1968
*SR. 77	77th meeting	20 May 1968

SECURITY COUNCIL

Official Records

21st YEAR (1966)

Supplements (All texts bilingual - E & F)

- for Jul, Aug and Sep. 1966.
  Apr 1968. xxi, 149 p. Printed. $U.S. 2.50 (or equivalent in other currencies).
  Includes check list of documents issued during the period covered with information on their re-publication.

22nd YEAR (1967)

Supplements (All texts bilingual - E & F)

- for Apr, May and Jun 1967.
  Mar 1968. xxv, 309 p. Printed. $U.S. 6.00 (or equivalent in other currencies).
  Includes check list of documents issued during the period covered with information on their republication.

Council Documents

General Series

S/7781/Add. 5. Report by the Secretary-General in pursuance of resolution 232 (1966) adopted by the Security Council at its 1340th meeting on 16 Dec 1966. 13 Jun 1968. [100] p., including annexes.
Concerns question of Southern Rhodesia.

S/7930/Add. 69. Supplemental information. 22 May 1968. 2 p.

--/Add. 70. 14 Jun 1968. 2 p.
Concerns Middle East situation.

--/Add. 71. 17 Jun 1968. 1 p.

S/8357/Add. 24. Question of South West Africa. Report of the Secretary-General. 23 May 1968. 3 p.
Also issued as A/7045/Add. 24.
Concerns South West Africa question.

--/Add. 25. 6 Jun 1968. 2 p.
Also issued as A/7045/Add. 25.

Checklist Section of the *United Nations Documents Index*

Index to Speeches Section of the *United Nations Documents Index*

duced for each meeting day of the Assembly and numbered consecutively. Most libraries file these together for a session, thus by checking the bound volumes of *Official Records* for the 21st General Assembly Session, and looking for the numbers referred to, you could read Andrei Gromyko's and Nicolai Federenko's blast at U.S. aggression in Vietnam. The other references in the entry, e.g., "I: 1473," refer to meetings of various committees of the General Assembly rather than to plenary meetings.

Also reproduced is the page from the "Subject Index" section for the 21st Session which relates to the "Vietnam Situation." Through this you could find out what any or all member representatives had to say on Vietnam.

(3) As noted above, the *United Nations Documents Index* began publication only in 1950, four years after the formation of the UN. For an approach to documents and publications of the 1946–1949 period, one must use a series of indexes, called *Checklists of United Nations Documents,* in which the documents of each organ are listed separately.

There are many other bibliographies and reference tools useful in connection with United Nations publications, but the three listed are basic. If the student learns to use these, he should be able to exploit UN publications and documents without great difficulty.

V. SPECIALIZED AGENCIES RELATED TO THE UNITED NATIONS

Over the years a number of intergovernmental organizations have developed in affiliation with the United Nations. All of these agencies issue documents and publications of their own, and some of them have networks of depository libraries. With the exception of the United Nations Educational, Scientific and Cultural Organization (UNESCO), library holdings of the materials emanating from these agencies are likely to be rather incomplete.

Prior to 1963, the documents and publications of most of these agencies were listed and indexed in the *United Nations Documents Index,* providing convenient bibliographic access to them. Beginning with 1963, this coverage was dropped, and since that date it is necessary to use publications lists or indexes issued by the specialized agencies themselves. Some of their most important publications,

EZUELA and GUYANA
undaries

Documents
   A/6325 United Kingdom and Venezuela. Letter,
   2 May, transmitting text of an Agreement
   signed in Geneva on 17 Feb, between the United Kingdom, in consultation with the Government of British Guiana and Venezuela concerning the frontier between British Guiana
   and Venezuela

Statements in General Debate
   Plenary: Meetings 1409 (Venezuela), 1424 (Venezuela), 1447 (Guyana, Venezuela)

OSTA, STEPHAN (Austria)
ography A/6360

D, MAURICE (France)
ography A/C.5/1084

GIN ISLANDS (BRITISH)
elf-government or independence (agenda item 23)
   GA resolution 2069 (XX)

Documents
   A/6300/Add.10 Special Cttee on the Situation with
   Regard to the Implementation of the Declaration on the Granting of Independence to
   Colonial Countries and Peoples. Report,
   chap. XXII
   A/C.4/L.866 Algeria, Burundi, Congo (Democratic Republic), Ethiopia, Ghana, India, Indonesia, Iraq, Kenya, Kuwait, Libya, Mali, Mauritania, Pakistan, Saudi Arabia, Sierra Leone, Somalia, Sudan, Syria, Uganda, United
   Arab Republic, United Republic of Tanzania,
   Yemen, Yugoslavia, Zambia. Draft resolution

Discussion in 4th Cttee: Meetings 1675, 1679
   A/6628 Report

Discussion in Plenary: Meeting 1500
   Draft resolution II in A/6628, reaffirming the ina-
   lienable right of the peoples of the Territory to self-determination and independence,
   reiterating inter alia that the establishment
   of military bases in the Territory is incom-
   patible with the principles of the Charter
   and of the GA resolution 1514 (XV), and urging
   the administering Power to allow United Nations visiting missions to visit the Territory,
   adopted by recorded vote (93-0-24) as resolution 2232 (XXI)

GIN ISLANDS (UNITED STATES)
elf-government or independence (agenda item 23)
   GA resolution 2069 (XX)

Documents
   A/6300/Add.10 Special Cttee on the Situation with
   Regard to the Implementation of the Decla-
   ration on the Granting of Independence to
   Colonial Countries and Peoples. Report,
   chap. XXII

VIRGIN ISLANDS (UNITED STATES) *(continued)*
-- self-government or independence *(continued)*

Documents (continued)
   A/C.4/L.866 Algeria, Burundi, Congo (Democratic Republic), Ethiopia, Ghana, India, Indonesia, Iraq, Kenya, Kuwait, Libya, Mali,
   Mauritania, Pakistan, Saudi Arabia, Sierra
   Leone, Somalia, Sudan, Syria, Uganda, United Arab Republic, United Republic of Tanzania, Yemen, Yugoslavia, Zambia. Draft
   resolution

Discussion in 4th Cttee: Meetings 1675, 1679
   A/6628 Report

Discussion in Plenary: Meeting 1500
   Draft resolution II in A/6628, reaffirming the in-
   alienable right of the peoples of the Territory to self-determination and independence,
   reiterating inter alia that the establishment
   of military bases in the Territory is incom-
   patible with the principles of the Charter and
   of the GA resolution 1514 (XV), and urging
   the administering Power to allow United Nations visiting missions to visit the Territory,
   adopted by recorded vote (93-0-24) as resolution 2232 (XXI)

VIET-NAM SITUATION

See also Force, Threat or use of
   Intervention: Declaration, 1965: implementation: status

Statements in General Debate
   2nd Cttee: Meetings 1024 (Poland), 1025 (USSR,
   United States), 1030 (Czechoslovakia), 1032
   (Bulgaria, Romania), 1034 (Hungary), 1037
   (Poland, USSR, United States)
   Plenary: Meetings 1411 (Philippines), 1412 (Cam-
   eroon, United States), 1413 (Canada, Guate-
   mala, USSR, United States), 1414 (Japan, Sen-
   egal), 1416 (Czechoslovakia, Ecuador, Malay-
   sia), 1418 (Australia, Ivory Coast, Mexico,
   Thailand), 1420 (Argentina, France, Peru,
   Singapore, United States), 1421 (Costa Rica,
   Kuwait, Uganda, Upper Volta, Uruluay), 1422
   (Albania, Denmark, Kenya, Turkey), 1423
   (Bulgaria, Burundi, Ethiopia, Finland, Nige-
   ria, Pakistan), 1424 (Burma, Chile, Indonesia, Netherlands, Venezuela), 1426 (Afghan-
   istan, Greece, Nepal), 1428 (Chad, Israel,
   Rwanda, Sierra Leone), 1430 (Austria, Mon-
   golia, Norway), 1432 (Belgium, Dahomey, In-
   dia, Yugoslavia), 1434 (Niger, Poland, Swe-
   den, Tunisia), 1435 (Cyprus, Ghana, Guinea,
   Liberia), 1436 (Malawi, Ukrainian SSR, United Kingdom), 1437 (Libya, United Republic of
   Tanzania), 1438 (China, Gabon, United Arab
   Republic), 1440 (Byelorussian SSR, Haiti,
   Iraq, Sudan), 1441 (Central African Republic,
   Italy, Morocco, Paraguay, Trinidad and Toba-
   go), 1442 (Dominican Republic, El Salvador,
   Romania), 1443 (Congo (Brazzaville), Iran,
   Mali, Saudi Arabia, Zambia), 1444 (Cambo-
   dia, Jamaica, Jordan), 1445 (Congo (Demo-
   cratic Republic), Maldive Islands, Yemen),
   1446 (Ceylon, Cuba, Hungary, Syria), 1447
   (Algeria, Honduras, Laos, New Zealand, So-
   malia, United States), 1464 (Zambia)

bject Index to the *United Nations Documents Index*

however, will be indexed in the periodical indexes discussed in Chapter 3, particularly in the *Public Affairs Information Service Bulletin*. The specialized agencies are: FAO, Food and Agricultural Organization; GATT, General Agreement on Tariffs and Trade; IAEA, International Atomic Energy Agency; IBRD or World Bank, International Bank for Reconstruction and Development; ICAO, International Civil Aviation Organization; IDA, International Development Association; IFC, International Finance Corporation; ILO, International Labour Organisation; IMCO, Inter-Governmental Maritime Consultative Organization; IMF or FUND, International Monetary Fund; ITU, International Telecommunication Union; UNESCO, United Nations Educational, Scientific and Cultural Organization; UPU, Universal Postal Union; WHO, World Health Organization; WMO, World Meteorological Organization.

VI. OTHER INTERNATIONAL ORGANIZATIONS

There are many international organizations outside the UN structure, such as the European Economic Community, the Council of Europe, NATO, etc., which issue publications of political science interest. Most of these issue lists or bibliographies of their own publications, though bibliographic control in this area is grossly inadequate. In the United States, perhaps the publications of the Organization of American States are the most readily available. The OAS maintains a system of depository libraries, and since 1961 OAS documents and publications have been available in microform. OAS materials may be located through its bibliography and index, the *Documentos Oficiales de la Organización de Los Estados Americanos* (Washington: Union Panamerica, 1963). Also, each quarterly issue of the *Inter-American Review of Bibliography* (Washington: Pan American Union, 1951–   ) lists current OAS publications.

Additional Information—Much more detailed information on how to locate and use United Nations documents and publications will be found in:

(1) Brimmer, Brenda, et al. *A Guide to the Use of United Nations Publications*. Dobbs Ferry, N.Y.: Oceana, 1962.

(2) Patch, William. *The Use of United Nations Documents*. Urbana: Univ. of Illinois Lib. Sch., Occasional Paper No. 64, March, 1962.

The bibliographical apparatus available for the use of League of Nations publications is described fully in Hans Aufricht, *Guide to League of Nations Publications, 1920–1947*. New York: AMS Press, 1951.

Chapter 7

State Government
Publications

I. AVAILABILITY AND TREATMENT IN LIBRARIES

No one knows how many publications are issued each year by the 50 state governments. Students in an increasingly quantitative discipline such as political science may be disturbed by such imprecision, so let us estimate the total at 30,000 per year. This output will be of particular interest to students of state government and public administration, and it provides a valuable data source, very little exploited to date, for comparative studies in many areas of political science.

In each state one library, usually the State Library or the leading university library, will attempt to maintain a comprehensive collection of the publications of that state. Only a few states have depository networks which insure good collections in a number of libraries throughout the state. Acquisition of publications from other states is a problematic affair, though many large libraries do attempt to collect them systematically by exchange agreements or other methods. Take it from one who has made the attempt, however, that this is about the most frustrating work librarians can find. It is said that American state governments have lost their independence and "sovereignty." When it comes to distributing their documents and publications, they are as cagey as any nation-state guarding its balance of payments.

The paragraph above implies that access to state publications will not be easy. The matter may as well be put forthrightly: attempting to get hold of state publications on any extensive basis, particularly from states other than your own, is a sure cure for dandruff. The Kansas student (for which read your own state) would do well not to pick a research topic requiring much use of Hawaiian state documents, unless he is independently wealthy and wants to take a long trip.

In recent years, however, this situation has been improved somewhat by the development of a large collection of state documents by the Center for Research Libraries in Chicago. Since 1952 the Center has attempted to acquire publications from all states as comprehensively as possible, and its holdings are available via interlibrary loan.

II. INDEXES TO STATE PUBLICATIONS

(1) *Monthly Checklist of State Publications.* Washington: Govt. Printing Off., 1910– . There is no single, complete list of all state documents, but this *Checklist* issued by the Library of Congress is the most extensive listing available. About 20,000 publications are listed each year, arranged alphabetically by state, with an annual index. Publications issued by regional organizations and associations of state officials are listed in a special section.

(2) *Legislative Research Checklist.* Chicago: Council of State Goverments, 1947– . This lists, by subject, studies underway or recently completed by legislative research agencies, study commissions, and legislative committees in the various states. The Falls City Microcard Co. of Louisville, Kentucky, sells microcards of all publications listed in this quarterly *Checklist.*

(3) Most states issue lists of their own publications on a quarterly or annual basis. Some, such as California's, are very complete and up-to-date. Generally, these are the most complete lists of publications for each state and may include items not listed in the two indexes above.

III. RECORDS OF THE STATES OF THE UNITED STATES

This is a massive collection, consisting of 1,765 reels of microfilm, containing the official public records of the American states from the earliest colonial records up to the Civil War period. Assembled by Professor William Sumner Jenkins of the University of North Carolina as a joint enterprise of that university and the Library of Congress, the collection contains legislative, statutory, constitutional, and other records of all the states for this lengthy period.

A Guide to the Microfilm Collection of Early State Records. Washington: Lib. of Congress, 1950, and *Supplement,* 1951. Compiled by Professor Jenkins to serve as an index to the collection. For a more detailed description of the format and content of the *Records,* see William S. Jenkins and Frederick Kirk, "Records of the States of the United States: a microfilm compilation," in the *Unesco Bulletin for Libraries,* March–April, 1965.

Additional Information—Though now dated, Jerome K. Wilcox's *Manual on the Use of State Publications* (Chicago: American Lib. Assn., 1940) remains the most comprehensive treatment of this subject. Ernst Posner's *American State Archives* (Chicago: Univ. of Chicago Press, 1964) describes the archival programs of each state and provides leads to the availability of unpublished materials.

Chapter 8

Statistical Sources

In recent years much political science research increasingly has required access to detailed statistical data. Unfortunately, available resources have not kept pace with these new demands. Much of the work of statistical data-gathering is done by governments, and while these have been very responsive to the needs of businessmen, economists, and even sociologists, they have paid little attention to the requirements of the political scientist. The U.S. government, for example, runs the most massive statistical program in the world. From its output it is a fairly simple matter to find out the annual receipts of pool halls and bowling alleys in Great Falls, Montana ($695,000); the number of chickens over four months of age in Sagadahoc County, Maine (21,025); or the number of brassieres shipped annually by American manufacturers (203,628,000). The student wanting to know the number of votes received by Richard Nixon in Mesa, Arizona, in 1968, however, will look in vain, at least in the government's statistical output.

Despite serious gaps, still there are many statistical sources of great value to the political scientist. The data are scattered throughout a great variety of reference books, documents, and other sources, are not well indexed, and are rather difficult to locate. Consequently this is an area, like government documents, in which the student may require considerable assistance from the library staff. Some of the more important data sources are listed and described below, along with leads to additional sources.

I. GOVERNMENT DOCUMENTS AS STATISTICAL DATA SOURCES

Though statistical data, in vast scope and depth, are scattered throughout thousands of government publications, the basic starting point for most searches is the *Statistical Abstract of the United States* (Washington: Govt. Printing Off., 1878–). This annual compendium brings together in one volume the major statistical sources produced by the federal government. It is divided into sections on Population, Education, Elections, Communications, etc. The 1968 volume contains over 1,200 separate tables packed with data. The emphasis is on recent national data, though many tables give extended time series and regional or state breakdowns. The *Statistical Abstract* is both a useful data source in itself and a "lead" to more detailed data. The "headnotes" at the top of most tables refer to *Historical Statistics of the United States, Colonial Times to 1957* (Washington: Govt. Printing Off., 1960) which contains a compilation of more than 8,000 statistical time series, largely annual, on American social and economic development. The "source notes" at the bottom of most tables refer to specific publications, such as census reports, other statistical compendia, and periodicals, which will contain more detailed or more recent data.

To illustrate the use of the *Statistical Abstract,* suppose you want to pin down the amount of U.S. economic assistance to Thailand in recent years. You can approach this in several ways through the index to the *Abstract.* Under "Thailand," for example, you find a cross reference reading: "See Foreign countries." Under the heading "Foreign countries" you find a sub-heading reading "Aid by U.S. Government" which refers you to pages 797–800 of the 1968 volume. On page 799 you find a table on "Major U.S. Government Foreign Assistance" (see illustration on the following page) which indicates that U.S. aid to Thailand totalled $424 million in the postwar period from July 1, 1945 through December 31, 1967. The table also shows the data, by year, from 1961 through 1967. Suppose you want to go further, however, and both bring the data up to date and find a breakdown by type of aid. The source note at the bottom of the page refers to a publication by the Department of Commerce entitled *Foreign Grants and Credits by the United States Government.* The source notes to adjacent tables in the *Abstract* refer to

No. **1209.** MAJOR U.S. GOVERNMENT FOREIGN ASSISTANCE, NET, BY COUNTRY: 1945 TO 1967—Continued

[In millions of dollars]

TYPE AND COUNTRY	Post-war period [1]	July 1945-Dec. 1960	1961	1962	1963	1964	1965	1966	1967 (prel.)
Far East and Pacific	16,490	11,019	748	775	776	567	655	958	991
Australia	190	−12	18	−6	−14	−1	25	27	153
Burma	101	73	4	3	10	5	3	2	1
Cambodia [8]	256	184	24	20	20	7	2	(Z)	(Z)
China (Taiwan)	2,188	1,748	119	82	76	45	49	31	38
Hong Kong	40	22	6	3	5	(−Z)	2	1	1
Indonesia	748	434	54	89	78	32	−4	26	40
Japan	2,581	2,532	26	57	32	−49	−57	47	−6
Korea, Republic of	4,230	2,841	230	238	240	158	165	165	193
Laos [8]	548	225	51	30	32	39	58	55	58
Malaysia	41	3	2	12	7	2	4	4	6
New Zealand	19	11	−2	−1	−1	−2	−1	21	−6
Philippines	1,184	987	12	26	11	49	45	22	33
Ryukyu Islands	337	246	5	11	8	22	19	12	15
Thailand	424	230	29	31	29	18	25	21	40
Trust Territory of the Pacific Islands	154	56	6	8	18	11	18	16	20
Viet-Nam [8]	3,229	1,291	151	157	212	221	300	499	398
Other [9] and unspecified	220	148	13	16	14	9	4	9	7
Western Hemisphere	6,971	2,655	710	587	576	447	632	720	644
Argentina	356	260	41	66	11	5	−3	−3	−21
Bolivia	398	191	23	29	45	33	30	22	24
Brazil	2,030	737	270	159	139	213	149	226	138
Canada	24	−7	–	–	–	(Z)	(Z)	–	31
Chile	875	217	122	88	111	96	101	87	53
Columbia	558	176	53	45	69	38	34	59	84
Costa Rica	118	51	7	9	7	10	14	10	11
Cuba	41	40	(Z)	(−Z)	(Z)	–	(Z)	–	–
Dominican Republic	284	(Z)	(Z)	22	48	22	79	53	60
Ecuador	172	52	11	12	14	17	17	21	28
El Salvador	84	10	8	6	11	10	11	17	11
Guatemala	180	104	14	9	10	9	11	7	15
Guyana	18	1	1	1	1	1	3	3	7
Haiti	102	67	14	5	3	3	5	3	3
Honduras	69	25	8	4	5	4	10	7	6
Jamaica	33	4	1	2	3	3	4	5	10
Mexico	506	334	83	21	−18	−55	38	54	49
Nicaragua	87	30	9	7	7	7	7	10	9
Panama	150	43	9	11	19	10	21	21	17
Paraguay	73	33	10	4	9	7	5	4	2
Peru	306	216	−20	5	4	17	32	28	24
Surinam	5	2	1	1	(Z)	(Z)	1	(Z)	(Z)
Trinidad and Tobago	43	1	(Z)	(Z)	9	8	17	6	2
Uruguay	68	43	3	4	8	(Z)	2	4	4
Venezuela	235	14	32	64	43	−40	38	39	46
Other [10] and unspecified	155	11	10	12	19	26	9	37	31
Other international organizations and unspecified areas	2,933	1,482	98	193	175	157	189	300	338

- Represents zero. NA Not available. Z Less than $500,000 or net minus (−) of less than $500,000.
[1] July 1, 1945, through Dec. 31, 1967. All lend-lease and conversions of prior grants to credits from V-J Day (Sept. 2, 1945). For additional details on immediate postwar period, see prior editions of the *Statistical Abstract*.
[2] Beginning 1964, Defense Dept. transactions estimated.
[3] Comprises Liechtenstein, Malta, San Marino, Switzerland, European Productivity Agency, North Atlantic Treaty Organization, and former Organization for European Economic Cooperation.
[4] United Nations Relief and Works Agency for Palestine refugees. [5] Comprises Aden, Bahrain, and Kuwait.
[6] Formerly known as Congo (Leopoldville).
[7] Comprises Botswana, British Islands East of Africa, Burundi, Canary Islands, Central African Republic, Chad, Congo (Brazzaville), French Somaliland, Gabon, Gambia, Lesotho, Malawi, Mauritania, Niger, Rwanda, St. Helena, Seychelles and dependencies, South West Africa, Southern Rhodesia, Swaziland, Upper Volta, Zambia, and unspecified Portuguese, French, and Spanish Africa.
[8] Separate data for Cambodia, Laos, and Viet-Nam became available during 1954. For earlier periods, total data were shown as Indochina (see footnote 9). Some unspecified transactions occurred in 1955 and 1956.
[9] Comprises British Solomon Islands, Fiji Islands, Indochina (see footnote 8), Macao, New Caledonia, Singapore, Tonga Islands, and Western Samoa.
[10] Comprises Bahamas, Barbados, British Honduras, British Virgin Islands, Central American Bank for Economic Integration, French Guiana, French West Indies, Inter-American Institute of Agricultural Sciences, Organization of American States, and Pan American Health Organization.

Source: Dept. of Commerce, Office of Business Economics; periodic report, *Foreign Grants and Credits by the United States Government*.

various publications of the Agency for International Development which contain data on foreign aid. As discussed in Chapter 5, you could check the *Monthly Catalog of U.S. Government Publications* and locate the most recent issues of these publications. In them you would find more recent data on U.S. aid to Thailand as well as breakdowns by type of aid.

Two other statistical compendia, issued as supplements to the *Statistical Abstract,* also are useful sources:

U.S. Bureau of the Census. *County and City Data Book.* Washington: Govt. Printing Off., 1949– . Published in 1949, 1952, 1956, 1962, with the latest edition issued in 1967, this contains selected statistical series, based on census data, for each county in the U.S., standard metropolitan statistical areas, and cities with more than 25,000 population. More than 140 items are presented for each unit.

U.S. Bureau of the Census. *Congressional District Data Book* (*Districts of the 88th Congress.*) Washington: Govt. Printing Off., 1963. Contains 254 statistical items, taken from census data, for each Congressional district. The latest edition is based on districts of the 88th Congress, but there are supplements for those states which have redistricted since 1962.

The various series of census reports constitute the most detailed statistical sources on the American society and economy. The best known of these is the *Census of Population,* last taken in 1960. Final reports for this census make a stack of publications 13 feet high, giving a rough idea of the detailed data reported. Other census series, less well-known but equally important for the subject areas covered are the Census of Agriculture, of Business, of Governments, of Housing, of Manufacturing, of Mineral Industries and of Transportation.

At first glance, some of these might seem of little relevance to the political science student. But in one case, at least, the *Census of Mineral Industries* proved to have considerable explanatory power. A student was attempting to analyze the Congressional performance of Representative Wilbur Mills of Arkansas. He found that Mills was a consistent "free-trader," or low tariff man, with one puzzling exception. Mills exhibited great concern about foreign imports of manganese or manganese ore and wanted the tariff rate on this commodity raised. Somewhat paradoxically, at the same time he was rather critical of Anaconda Copper Company, the largest manganese mining company in the country, with over 500 employees. A check of the *Census of Mineral Industries* disclosed that there were 15 manganese mining companies in Mills' district and that these mines produced over five percent of all manganese ore in the country. The Census also showed that, unlike Anaconda, these were very small companies, the largest employing only 49 men.

In addition to the major sources mentioned above, federal agencies grind out thousands of publications each year containing statistical data. The student who must do intensive work in this area might want to consult:

Andriot, John L. *Guide to United States Government Statistics.* 3rd ed. Arlington, Va.: Documents Index, 1961. This attempts "to provide a comprehensive guide to statistical contents of the voluminous output of Federal publications." Andriot lists 1,777 such publications, giving a brief abstract of statistical data contained in each.

U.S. Bureau of the Budget. *Statistical Services of the United States Government.* rev. ed. Washington: Govt. Printing Off., 1968. This describes the statistical program of the government, with a list and description of the principal statistical publications of federal agencies.

U.S. Bureau of the Census. *Directory of Federal Statistics for States; a guide to sources.* Washington: Govt. Printing Off., 1967. "Intended as a comprehensive finding guide to available published sources of Federal statistics on social, political, and economic subjects." A subject listing of sources containing data on the state level.

U.S. Bureau of the Census. *Directory of Federal Statistics for Local Areas.* Washington: Govt. Printing Off., 1966. A finding guide to sources of federal statistics for metropolitan areas, counties, urban places, and other local areas.

II. STATISTICAL DATA ON FOREIGN COUNTRIES

Data on most foreign countries, particularly in the developing areas, are far less accessible than for the United States. In recent years, however, the United Nations, UNESCO and other international organizations have stimulated data-gathering in many countries and have produced various statistical compendia. Only a few of the more important ones are listed below; the student who needs to make intensive use of international statistical data sources should learn to use UN and other international documents.

Statistical Yearbook. New York: United Nations. Statistical Off., 1948– . Roughly the UN equivalent of the U.S. *Statistical Abstract.* Each volume contains sections on population, communications, national income, education, etc. The major problem with the *Yearbook,* as with most other international statistical compendia, is the frequent lack of comparability among data for various countries and the gaps in data for less-developed areas. Still, this is the best starting point, and some of its gaps can be filled by other sources listed in this section.

Compendium of Social Statistics: 1963. New York: United Nations, 1963. A joint publication of the UN, the International Labour Organisation and other international agencies, presenting data available as of November, 1962. The objective is to provide "basic statistical indicators required for describing the major aspects of the social situation in the world and the regions, as well as changes or trends in the levels of living over the decade ended 1960." The 1963 edition of this work was experimental, and it is expected that later editions will be published.

Demographic Yearbook. New York: United Nations. Statistical Off., 1948– . The best single world-wide source for data on population, mortality, natality, etc. The 1963 volume has a cumulative subject index covering all previous volumes.

World Communications. 4th ed. New York: Unesco Pubns. Center, 1964. A concise handbook on the development and diffusion of newspapers, radio, television and film in all countries. Might be of some help to the student who wants to follow up on Deutsch's work.

Monthly Bulletin of Statistics. New York: United Nations, 1947– . This keeps the sources listed above more or less up-to-date by providing recent data for many of the statistical series contained in those sources.

Ernst, Morris and Judith Posner, eds. *The Comparative International Almanac*. New York: Macmillan, 1967. Very brief economic, cultural and demographic data on 214 countries. Has a "ranking" section which ranks countries in terms of such variables as per capita annual income, literacy rate, suicide rate, newspaper circulation, and other communication and economic factors.

International Statistical Yearbook of Large Towns. The Hague: Intl. Statistical Inst., 1961– . Contains data on population, employment, communications, etc., for major European and a few non-European cities.

Many countries publish statistical yearbooks similar to the U.S. *Statistical Abstract*. If the student is looking for detailed data on one country, rather than comparable data on many countries, these yearbooks usually will be better sources than the publications listed above. A list of such yearbooks, by country, may be found on pages 377–387 of Constance M. Winchell, *Guide to Reference Books*, 8th ed. (Chicago: American Lib. Assn., 1967). *Statistical Sources*, described at the end of this chapter, also contains a listing of national statistical yearbooks. The most comprehensive list is Joyce Ball, ed., *Foreign Statistical Documents; a bibliography of general, international trade, and agricultural statistics, including holdings of the Stanford University Libraries*. Stanford, Calif.: Hoover Inst., Hoover Inst. Bibliographical Series, No. 28, 1967. This lists, by country, the statistical annuals and other publications of foreign governments.

In recent years the ferment in comparative politics has produced two novel statistical sources which go beyond simple presentation of raw data and into coding and correlation of variables:

Banks, Arthur S. and Robert B. Textor. *A Cross-Polity Survey*. Cambridge, Mass.: M.I.T. Press, 1963. This is, in effect, a computer printout containing analysis of 57 variables for 115 countries. In addition to the usual "hard" variables such as population, national product, etc., it attempts to code polities in terms of such "soft" variables as interest articulation by groups, freedom of association, interest aggregation by parties, etc.

Russet, Bruce M., et al. *World Handbook of Political and Social Indicators*. New Haven: Yale Univ. Press, 1964. Similar in many respects to Banks and Textor, but sticks more closely to "hard" variables and presents data on 75 such variables for 133 states and colonies.

Recent agitation by specialists in comparative politics may lead to some improvement in the production of statistical data on foreign areas. For some of the possibilities, see Richard L. Merritt and Stein Rokkan, *Comparing Nations; the use of quantitative data in cross-national research* (New Haven: Yale Univ. Press, 1966).

III. ELECTION STATISTICS

Much election data is buried in official or semi-official manuals or "blue books" issued by various states. The best guide to these is Charles Press and Oliver Williams, *State Manuals, Blue Books, and Election Results* (Berkeley: Inst. of Governmental Studies, Univ. of California, 1962). This lists manuals or blue books for each state, indicating the extent and type of election data reported, and should be consulted to supplement the sources listed below.

Despite considerable improvement in recent years, there remain many gaps in coverage of election data. Perhaps the most serious is the lack of easily accessible data below the county level. In any library which has the U.S. *Census of Housing,* it is not a difficult matter to find out how many houses on a specific block in Beverly Hills, California, lack flush toilets. Finding the vote division for a Presidential election in any Beverly Hills precinct, however, may require an on-site visit to the local election board. Another gap is the lack of reporting on Presidential voting by Congressional districts. Where county data are available, sometimes the district data can be built up, but this is a tedious business.

The Survey Research Center of the University of Michigan has a project underway which should greatly simplify research based upon aggregate election data. The Center has collected and is now key-punching all Presidential, Gubernatorial, and Senatorial votes, by county, from 1824 to the present. Congressional votes, by district, are being collected for a similar time span.

A few of the more important sources of election data are listed below. The best general discussion of this subject, however, is Walter Dean Burnham's paper, "Pilot Study; recovery of historical election data," done in 1962 for the Committee on Political Behavior of the

Social Science Research Council. And see also Walter Dean Burnham's *Sources of Historical Election Data; a preliminary bibliography*. East Lansing: Inst. for Community Development and Services, Michigan State Univ., 1963.

Scammon, Richard M., ed. *America Votes; a handbook of contemporary American election statistics*. Washington: Congressional Quarterly, Inc., 1956– . Seven volumes published to date. Presents data, by states, on Presidential, Senatorial, Congressional, and Gubernatorial elections from the late 1940's through 1968. Tables carry data down to county level (to ward level for some major cities) and give percentage breakdowns of votes by major parties. Accompanying maps show Congressional district, county, and some ward boundaries. The best general source for recent U.S. election data.

Scammon, Richard M., ed. *America at the Polls; a handbook of American Presidential election statistics, 1920–1964*. Pittsburgh, Pa.: Univ. of Pittsburgh Press, 1965. Contains data, by state and down to county level, for Presidential elections only.

U.S. Congress. House of Representatives. *Statistics of the Presidential and Congressional Election*. Washington: Govt. Printing Off., 1921– . The official tabulation prepared by the Clerk of the House of Representatives. Does not go below the state level for Presidential and Senatorial elections, or below district level for elections to the House.

Burnham, Walter Dean. *Presidential Ballots, 1836–1892*. Baltimore: Johns Hopkins Univ. Press, 1955. A county-by-county presentation of the Presidential vote for these years. Similar data up through the election of 1932 are contained in Edgar E. Robinson's *The Presidential Vote, 1896–1932* (Stanford, Calif.: Stanford Univ. Press, 1934) and for 1932 through 1944 in Robinson's *They Voted for Roosevelt* (Stanford, Calif.: Stanford Univ. Press, 1947).

Petersen, Svend. *A Statistical History of the American Presidential Elections*. New York: Frederick Ungar, 1963. Claims to be "the only publication that gives complete statistics on the American Presidential elections." Depends on what you mean by "complete." It is not really a depth source, since there is no breakdown below the state level. Most of the data here can be found in other sources, but one unique feature is a section showing the vote for each historical party by election and state. This is good for settling arguments; it shows, for example, that the high tide of the Communist Party in North Carolina came in 1936, when it got a total of 11 votes.

In recent years universities or research institutes in several states have published compilations of election data for their states, patterned more or less on *America Votes*. Many of these will go into more detail for a particular state than the general sources listed above. Though the listing may be incomplete, the following have come to the author's attention:

Arizona—Mason, Bruce B. *Arizona General Election Results, 1911–1960*. (Tempe: Bureau of Governmental Research, Arizona State Univ., 1961.)

California—Lee, Eugene C. *California Votes, 1928–1960; with 1962 supplement*. (Berkeley: Inst. of Governmental Studies, Univ. of California, 1963.)

Florida—Hartsfield, Annie M. and Elston G. Roady. *Florida Votes, 1920–1962*. (Tallahassee: Inst. of Governmental Research, Florida State Univ., 1963.)

Illinois—Gove, Samuel K. *Illinois Votes, 1900–1958; with 1960–1962 supplement*. (Urbana: Inst. of Government and Public Affairs, Univ. of Illinois, 1959.)

Indiana—Francis, Wayne L. and Sharon E. Doerner. *Indiana Votes; elections for United States Representative; elections for State General Assembly, 1922–1958*. (Bloomington: Bureau of Governmental Research, Indiana Univ., 1959.) See also, Robert J. Pitchell, *Indiana Votes; elections for Governor, 1852–1956; elections for United States Senator, 1914–1958*. (Bloomington: Bureau of Governmental Research, Indiana Univ., 1960.)

Kansas—Cabe, June G. and Charles A. Sullivant. *Kansas Votes; national elections, 1859–1956*. See also, Clarence J. Hein and Charles A. Sullivant, *Kansas Votes; gubernatorial elections, 1859–1956* and Herman D. Lujan, *Kansas Votes; national and statewide general elections, 1958–1964*. All three titles were published by the Governmental Research Center, University of Kansas.

Kentucky—Jewell, Malcolm. *Kentucky Votes.* (Lexington: Univ. of Kentucky Press, 1963.) Three volumes covering various elections from 1920 through 1962. See also, Jasper B. Shannon, *Presidential Politics in Kentucky, 1824–1948.* (Lexington: Bureau of Government Research, Univ. of Kentucky, 1950.)

Maryland—Wentworth, Evelyn. *Election Statistics in Maryland, 1934–1958.* (College Park: Bureau of Governmental Research, Univ. of Maryland, 1959.)

Mississippi—Abney, F. Glenn. *Mississippi Election Statistics, 1900–1967.* (University: Bureau of Governmental Research, Univ. of Mississippi, 1968.)

Montana—Waldron, Ellis L. *Montana Politics since 1864; an atlas of elections.* (Missoula: Montana State Univ. Press, 1958.)

Nevada—*Nevada Votes; votes cast in major election contests, 1910–1964.* (Reno: Bureau of Governmental Research, Univ. of Nevada, 1965.)

North Carolina—Matthews, Donald R. *North Carolina Votes.* (Chapel Hill: Univ. of North Carolina Press, 1962.) Data on national and state elections from 1868 through 1960.

Oklahoma—Benson, Oliver. *Oklahoma Votes, 1907–1962.* (Norman: Bureau of Government Research, Univ. of Oklahoma, 1964.) Also, Jack W. Strain, *Oklahoma Votes for Congress, 1907–1964.* (Norman: Bureau of Government Research, Univ. of Oklahoma, 1965.)

South Dakota—Clem, Alan L. *South Dakota Political Almanac; a presentation and analysis of election statistics, 1889–1960.* (Vermillion: Governmental Research Bureau, State Univ. of South Dakota, 1962.)

Texas—Marburger, Harold J. *Texas Elections, 1918–1954.* (Austin: Legislative Reference Division, Texas State Lib., 1956.) See also, *Texas Votes; selected general and special election statistics, 1944–1963.* (Austin: Inst. of Public Affairs, Univ. of Texas, 1964.)

Wisconsin—Donoghue, James R. *How Wisconsin Voted, 1848–1960.* (Madison: Bureau of Government, Univ. of Wisconsin, 1962.)

IV. FOREIGN ELECTION STATISTICS

Election data on foreign countries are considerably less accessible than for the United States and are scattered through newspapers, official publications, books and other sources. One general source of some value is the series entitled *A Review of Elections, 1954/58—* (London: Inst. of Electoral Research). This contains brief notes on the electoral system and parties in a number of countries, plus tables on national elections since 1954. The following provide greater detail on the areas or countries covered:

Inst. for the Comparative Study of Political Systems. *Election Factbooks.* Washington: The Institute. A series of brief election factbooks, containing data and analysis, on recent elections in Latin American countries. So far factbooks have appeared for Argentina, Bolivia, Brazil, Chile, Colombia, Costa Rica, the Dominican Republic, Guatemala, Jamaica, Nicaragua, Uruguay and Venezuela.

Mitchell, Brian R. *British Parliamentary Election Results, 1950–1964.* Cambridge, Eng.: Cambridge Univ. Press, 1966. Contains data, by constituency and election, showing total vote and percentage for each party candidate, plus figures on extent of participation. A brief bibliography lists other sources where data on British elections may be found.

Butler, David and Jennie Freeman. *British Political Facts, 1900–1967.* rev. ed. London: Macmillan, 1968. Has a brief section on general and by-elections from 1900 through 1966. Cites additional sources which contain more detailed data.

Kinnear, Michael. *The British Voter: an atlas and survey since 1885.* Ithaca, N.Y.: Cornell Univ. Press, 1968. Presents statistical data and analysis on each British general election since 1885, plus special analyses of the realignment in party support during the 1920's. Contains 55 electoral maps keyed to parliamentary constituencies. Emphasis is on social and economic factors underlying political trends.

Scarrow, Howard A. *Canada Votes; a handbook of federal and provincial election data.* New Orleans: Hauser, 1962. Contains data on federal general elections from 1873 through 1958 and on provincial elections from 1920 through 1960.

The International Committee for Social Sciences Documentation is planning a series of *International Guides to Electoral Statistics*. The first volume, covering 15 Western European countries, is to be published shortly; later volumes will cover non-European areas. When completed, these guides should alleviate some of the problems in locating foreign election data.

V. OTHER SOURCES OF STATISTICAL DATA

Statistical data are generated in massive quantity on many subjects by commercial agencies, trade associations, universities, research organizations, foundations, etc. The best general guide to this output is Paul Wasserman's *Statistical Sources*. 2nd ed. (Detroit: Gale, 1966). This is a subject index to primary sources of statistical data, citing the original publications in which the data appear. The listing of "Primary Statistics Sources" under each country leads to the most important national statistical yearbooks.

Chapter 9

English-Language
Translations of
Foreign Sources

Many political science students, and not only those in "area study" programs, need to use foreign-language materials. Access to these is severely limited by the language barrier and by the relative lack of foreign sources, especially in non-Western languages, in libraries.

Within the last decade or so much has been done to overcome these obstacles by centralized acquisition and translation of foreign-language materials. The greatest impetus in this direction has come from the federal government, and—given the government's postwar preoccupations—it is not surprising that the major emphasis has been upon translation of Soviet, Chinese, and other Communist sources. Translations are issued, however, by a variety of producers, both governmental and private, on many subjects from many languages. Since sources, coverage, format and other factors vary, and particularly since translations are not well-indexed, location and use of this material may be rather difficult. The major translations currently published which are of political science interest are listed and described below. Given the rapid developments in this field, this listing soon will be out-of-date. Few libraries will have all the translations mentioned, though some large libraries with specialized collec-

tions on Soviet studies, Chinese studies, etc., may have additional
materials not listed here.

I. GENERAL SOURCES

U.S. Joint Publications Research Service Reports. Washington: Joint
Publications Research Service, 1957– . The Joint Publications Research Service (JPRS) is a government service agency centered in the
Commerce Department which produces translations of Soviet, Chinese,
other Communist, and some non-Communist sources. Its translation
program has reached massive proportions. Since its inception in 1957,
JPRS has issued almost two million pages of translations, comprising
over 41,000 numbered reports, or an estimated 130,000 separate
articles. At present over 500 reports are issued each month, with an
annual output of around 250,000 pages. Approximately 70% of the
JPRS output is related to social science subjects, and much of this is of
direct political science interest. JPRS claims that its reports "represent
the largest body of current translations—on numerous subjects and
from various languages—available to the government and to the general public." JPRS reports fall into three categories:

(a) Serial Publications—These constitute approximately two-thirds
of total output. The serial reports are compiled on the basis of a common source or subject matter. An example of a "common source"
series is the *Translations from Kommunist,* the theoretical journal of
the Soviet party, which JPRS began translating in 1960. Most series
are based on common subject matter; a number of articles, documents, etc., will be translated from various sources and grouped by
JPRS under collective titles such as *Soviet Military Translations, Political Translations on Eastern Europe, Translations of Political and
Sociological Information on Communist China,* etc. At present JPRS
issues 95 serial titles; 42 deal with the USSR, 25 with Eastern Europe,
9 with Communist China, 7 with Asia excluding China, 3 with Latin
America, 2 on the Near East and Africa, and 7 on International Developments. The latter series deals primarily with Communist parties
outside what used to be called the "Sino-Soviet Bloc." The JPRS output shifts somewhat to reflect current interests and concerns of the
government; in recent years there has been a considerable increase in
translation of North Vietnamese sources.

(b) Ad Hoc Translations—This category contains translations of
single articles or documents which do not fit into the series described

above. An example would be the translation of Ulbricht's report to the Sixth East German Party Congress.

(c) Books—These translations are similar to the *ad hoc* category, the difference being mainly one of length. One example is the translation of a 321-page book on Africa by the late Professor I. I. Potekhin, Director of the Soviet Africa Institute.

Joint Publications Research Service translations are available from three sources:

(a) by series subscription or single reports, in hard copy or microfiche, from the Clearinghouse for Federal Scientific and Technical Information, Springfield, Va. 22151. This is the best source for an individual who does not have access to a library collection of JPRS reports, or who wants an occasional report for personal use.

(b) by series subscription on microfilm or microfiche from Research and Microfilm Publications, Inc., 866 Third Ave., New York, N.Y. 10022.

(c) by subscription, for total output only, on Microprint from the Readex Microprint Corporation, 5 Union Square, New York, N.Y., 10003. (See Chapter 5 of this guide for information on how to locate materials in the Readex Microprint edition of government publications.)

Even when a library has JPRS translations, bibliographic access to them is rather difficult. Until recently the *Monthly Catalog of United States Government Publications* provided at least some subject approaches by which translations could be located. The *Monthly Catalog* still lists JPRS reports, but by series title only, and since early 1965 its subject indexing of the translations has become almost useless. However, beginning with January, 1968, JPRS translations are listed, abstracted, and indexed in *U.S. Government Research & Development Reports,* described in Chapter 5.

Since 1962, Research and Microfilm, Inc., has issued a monthly *Bibliography-Index to U.S. JPRS Research Translations* which does provide subject indexing. The *Bibliography-Index* is published in four separate sections on the *Soviet Union, East Europe, China and Asia,* and *International Developments.* Each section carries the same subject index which covers all JPRS social science translations. Since January, 1966, a separate publication, the *Subject Index to U.S. JPRS Translations,* has been issued semiannually; this is a cumulation of the index which appears in the four sections listed above.

U.S. Foreign Broadcast Information Service. *Daily Report: Foreign Radio Broadcasts,* 1947– . The Daily Report carries translations of radio broadcasts, in full or summary form, on a world-wide basis, including Radio Moscow, Peking, Havana, etc. Each report is divided into four sections on Latin America; the Middle East, Africa and Western Europe; USSR and Eastern Europe; and the Far East. This is the source for those newspaper articles beginning: "Broadcasts from Hanoi yesterday indicated. . . ." There is no index to the *Daily Report,* making exhaustive searching necessary to fully exploit the material.

British Broadcasting Corporation. *Summary of World Broadcasts.* Reading, Eng.: British Broadcasting Corp. Monitoring Service, 1947– . The BBC has published summaries of world broadcasts since 1939, and since 1947 under the present title. Though coverage and format have varied, at present the *Summary* consists of four parts (USSR, Eastern Europe, Far East, Middle East) with each part containing an "Introduction" and divided into sections on International Affairs (further subdivided by region), Internal Affairs, and Special Occasions. There appears to be considerable duplication between this and the Foreign Broadcast Information Service *Daily Report.*

II. SOVIET SOURCES

Current Digest of the Soviet Press. New York: Joint Committee on Slavic Studies, 1949– . A weekly periodical containing full translations or summaries of articles in the Soviet press. In addition to full coverage of *Pravda* and *Izvestia,* it contains selections from over 40 other newspapers and periodicals. There is a quarterly subject index, providing good bibliographic access to the material.

Digest of the Soviet Ukrainian Press. New York: PROLOG Research and Publishing Associates, 1957– . Published monthly, with an annual index, containing full translations or summaries from major Ukrainian newspapers and periodicals.

Soviet Law and Government. White Plains, N.Y.: Intl. Arts and Sciences Press, 1962– . Published quarterly and contains complete translations or selections from major Soviet specialist journals dealing with law and government. "Articles are selected which best reflect developments in Soviet law and government and which are of most interest to those professionally concerned with these fields." The same publisher issues *Soviet Statutes and Decisions* (1962–   ), which translates major new Soviet legislation and court decisions. A third translation periodical, *Soviet Studies in World Economics and Politics,* is scheduled to begin publication shortly.

Soviet Periodical Abstracts. White Plains, N.Y.: Slavic Language Research Inst., 1961–   . A quarterly abstract journal divided into two sections:

   Soviet Society—selects and abstracts articles published in current Russian periodicals on education, sociology, public administration, etc. Contains abstracts only, but cites location of full translations when these are available.

   Asia, Africa, and Latin America—selects and abstracts articles which present the Soviet view on political and social developments in these areas.

Mizan; USSR-China-Africa-Asia. London: Central Asian Research Center, 1959–   . This monthly periodical usually does not provide full translations, but summarizes and analyzes Soviet and Chinese writing on other areas. Beginning January, 1966, two supplements were issued: *Supplement A—Soviet and Chinese Reports on the Middle East and Africa* and *Supplement B—Soviet and Chinese Reports on Southeast Asia.*

Reprints from the Soviet Press. New York: Compass Pubns., 1963–   . Full translations of important speeches, reports and statements by Soviet leaders and joint communiques between the USSR and other countries. Prior to 1966, title was *Current Soviet Documents.*

III. CHINESE SOURCES

Since the early 1950's the American Consulate in Hong Kong has conducted an extensive program of acquiring and translating publications from Communist China. It issues three major translation series:

   Survey of China Mainland Press, 1950–   . Contains full translations or summaries of articles appearing in Chinese Communist newspapers or releases from news agencies. Issued several times a week, generally on a daily basis. Over 4,300 numbers have appeared to date, with each number now divided into "National" and "Foreign Relations" sections and running from 30 to 40 pages.

Selections from China Mainland Magazines, 1955– . Translations of articles in Chinese Communist periodicals. Over 600 numbers have been issued. Until June, 1960, this appeared under the title *Extracts from China Mainland Magazines.*

Current Background, 1950– . Coverage varies, but each number usually focuses on a particular subject and contains translations from various sources dealing with that subject. Issued irregularly, usually three to four times a month, with over 1,900 numbers to date.

The American Consulate also publishes a combined index to translations appearing in these three series.

Union Research Service. Hong Kong: Union Research Inst., 1955– . A semi-weekly publication produced by a private agency in Hong Kong. Each issue usually covers a particular subject, containing translations from a variety of Chinese Communist sources. Emphasis is upon provincial newspapers and other sources not covered by the U.S. Consulate series.

Peking Review. Peking: Peking Review, 1958– . A weekly Chinese Communist propaganda periodical, which also carries translations of major Chinese statements and communiques. Has translated all of the Chinese polemical articles and letters in the Sino-Soviet debate, as well as Soviet responses.

China News Analysis. Hong Kong: China News Analysis, 1953– . A weekly newsletter summarizing events and conditions in China and other Asian countries. Frequently contains analytical summaries of the Chinese press, a recent example being "The Press of Peking on Vietnam."

Chinese Law and Government. White Plains, N.Y.: Intl. Arts and Sciences Press, 1968– . Contains translations of articles and documents, primarily from Chinese specialist journals, on government and legal systems of Communist China.

IV. OTHER SOURCES

American Embassy Press Translations—Many American embassies or U.S. Information Service posts produce press translations from the countries to which they are accredited. These follow pretty much the pattern of the Hong Kong Consulate series on China, though most of them are far less extensive. In library terminology, these translations are "fugitive," meaning they are very difficult to acquire. Though few libraries will have them, the following series have been identified and are listed for the record, by country:

Afghanistan: *Daily Press Digest.*
Argentina: *Daily Digest of the Local Press.*
Austria: *Daily Press Summary.*
Brazil: *Rio Press Summary.*
Bulgaria: *Press Summary.*
Burma: *Weekly Review of Rangoon Chinese Press.*
China (Taiwan): *Press and Publications Summary.*
Denmark: *News of the Day.*
East Europe: *East Europe Daily Press Report*
   (covers several countries).
Finland: *Summary of the Finnish Press.*
Germany: *Berlin Press Commentaries.*
Greece: *Daily News Review.*
       Editorial Opinion from the Athenian Press.
       News Review from Sunday's Athenian Press.
Guatemala: *Press Digest.*
Iceland: *Translations of Icelandic Newspapers.*
India: *Survey of Indian Press Comment.*
       Bengali Press Opinion Survey.
       Weekly Press Opinion Survey.
       Survey of South Indian Press Opinion.
Indonesia: *Translations of the Indonesian Press.*
Iran: *Tehran Press Review.*
Israel: *Hebrew Daily Press.*
       Summary of the Arab-Israeli Press.
Japan: *Daily Summary of the Japanese Press.*
       Summaries of Selected Japanese Magazines.
       Trend of Japanese Magazines.
Jordan: *Arabic Press Translations.*
Korea: *Daily Press Translations.*
Lebanon: *Lebanese Press Review.*
Libya: *Arabic Press Summary.*
Norway: *Norwegian Press Review.*
Pakistan: *Digest of the Karachi Vernacular Press.*

Poland: *Polish News Bulletin.*
Rumania: *Rumanian Press Review.*
South Vietnam: *Saigon Press Analysis.*
Syria: *Daily Review of the Syrian Press.*
Thailand: *Summary of the Thai and Chinese Press.*
United Arab Republic: *Daily Review of the Arabic Press.*
Yugoslavia: *Summary of the Yugoslav Press.*

The German Tribune; a weekly review of the German Press. Hamburg: The German Tribune, 1962– . Contains full translations of articles appearing in leading West German newspapers.

Eastern European Studies in Law and Government. White Plains, N.Y.: Intl. Arts and Sciences Press, 1968– . A quarterly journal carrying translations, chiefly from scholarly or specialist periodicals published in Eastern Europe, on the politics, law and government of the countries in this area.

The Maghreb Digest: North African perspectives. Los Angeles: Sch. of Intl. Relations, Univ. of Southern California, 1963– . A monthly summary of political and economic events in North Africa, from the French and the Arabic-language periodicals of the region.

Thought; a journal of Afrikaans thinking for the English-speaking. Johannesburg: South African Inst. of Race Relations, 1955– . Summarizes articles and editorials in leading South African newspapers and periodicals.

SUMMARY

In addition to locating them bibliographically and physically, there are other problems in using translations such as those listed. They may be badly done and unfaithful to the original, hence specialists who command the requisite languages tend to be wary of them and prefer to work with the original sources. Anyone using translations also is dependent upon whatever criteria of selection were employed by those who produced them. For most students these problems can be safely ignored; your grade prospects will not be in jeopardy if you sprinkle liberal citations to "SCMP" or "JPRS" throughout your term papers.

It is said that, buried deep within the CIA headquarters outside Washington, there exist huge quantities of translations from all over the world, plus a highly sophisticated computer system known as WALNUT which retrieves them instantaneously. If so, gaining access to them is far harder than cracking walnuts with your teeth. When once queried on this by the author, a CIA librarian was uncommunicative to the point of taciturnity. If you have all the clearances, however, and can afford a trip to Washington, perhaps you can penetrate these mysteries.

PART B: *Bibliographies and Other Reference Sources*

Chapter 10

The Importance
of Bibliographies

The emphasis in this guide so far has been more upon "methods and procedures" of literature searching, or upon broad types of sources, than upon specific books, reference tools bibliographies, etc. Two reasons for such an emphasis are that any listing of specifics quickly becomes dated, and if the student learns the methods reasonably well, he can find his own way to specifics, and along the way he may discover many interesting things which he might otherwise miss. (For example, a bibliography issued as a government document yielded *The Girlwatcher's Manual,* a programmed text consisting of 200 film frames and 110 pages. To save the time of interested students, the manual is published by Graficroll Systems, Inc., 4215 Calavo Dr., La Mesa, California, and costs $4.95.)

In checking through the card catalog, in dragging through periodical indexes, and in using other library materials discussed in the foregoing chapters of this guide, the student in effect is compiling a bibliography of relevant sources on his particular subject. But this is a routine and preliminary step; presumably the student will want to get through the mechanics as quickly as possible and get down to the more substantive work of writing a paper. There is no point in compiling a bibliography if someone has already done the job for you, and for many subjects this will be the case, to a greater or lesser extent.

Suppose, for example, that you are writing a paper on some aspect of nationalism. If you can discover that Karl Deutsch has produced a 165-page bibliography entitled *An Interdisciplinary Bibliography on Nationalism, 1935–1953,* you can short-cut much of the routine work of literature searching. Therefore, it will pay to be on the lookout for bibliographies from the very beginning.

Though librarians might quibble about the over-simplification, basically there are three types of bibliographies:

Book-Length Bibliographies—In these cases the book itself is a bibliography; the Deutsch bibliography on nationalism is an example. In library card catalogs, book-length bibliographies have author, title, and subject cards exactly as other books. They may be located by the "form" sub-heading "Bibliography" which is added to the subject heading. The subject card for Deutsch's book reads (in red type), "Nationalism—Bibliography."

There are many book-length bibliographies relevant to political science, as the listings in the following chapters indicate. This seeming plenty is perhaps misleading, however, for there are serious gaps. For example, the literature on American political parties is voluminous. Weighed by the pound, there probably is more printed matter on this subject than any other single subject in the field of political science, and one might expect to find excellent bibliographies of this literature. Apparently, however, the most recent book-length bibliography on American parties was done in 1915 by the New York Public Library. There is a similar lack of coverage for the equally extensive literature on pressure groups. Despite many gaps, it will pay the student to check carefully to see if there is a book-length bibliography on his subject.

Bibliographies in Books—A "good bibliography" is part of the baggage of scholarship, which means that most books will themselves contain bibliographies, either in the form of appendices or bibliographical footnotes. Some authors do an exhaustive job in this respect, while others simply go through the motions, and it is not easy to locate good bibliographies of this type. The card catalog will be of some help. Most cards will contain "bibliographical notes" indicating if the book has a bibliography. Under the subject heading "Political parties," for example, there may be a card for Sigmund

Neumann's *Modern Political Parties; approaches to comparative politics*. The card will contain the note: "Bibliography, p. 425–446." The card for V. O. Key's *Parties, Politics, and Pressure Groups* has a note, "Bibliographical footnotes." Both books provide reasonably good listings of the relevant literature on political parties.

Bibliographical Articles—Many excellent bibliographies appear as articles in various political science journals. The student probably is most familiar with the bibliographical essays which appear from time to time in the *American Political Science Review*; similar articles are published in many other journals. The best approach to them is through the periodical indexes described in Chapter 3. Most of these will contain "form" sub-headings for bibliographical articles, just as the card catalog does for books.

Two sources provide a reasonably good listing of bibliographies in various forms:

Bibliographic Index. New York: Wilson, 1937– . This is a subject index to separately published bibliographies as well as bibliographies included in books and periodicals. Under the heading "Nationalism" in the *Index* for 1964, for example, one finds that Deutsch has supplemented his earlier book-length bibliography with a bibliographical appendix appearing on pages 132–150 of his book, *Nation-building,* which was published in 1963.

Besterman, Theodore. *A World Bibliography of Bibliographies*. 4th ed. 5 vs. Lausanne: Societas Bibliographica, 1966. A subject list of over 100,000 separately published bibliographies in all fields. Selective coverage of political science bibliographies, with emphasis on foreign-language bibliographies.

There will be many cases when no pre-existing bibliography in any form is available. The more esoteric and specialized the topic, in fact, the less likely is one to find a bibliographical "crutch." The student doing a paper on "Childhood political socialization among the Kurdish minority in Iraq" probably would waste his time looking for a bibliography; he will need a large Rockefeller grant for field research. For more standard topics, however, a brief search for pre-existing bibliographies is likely to pay large dividends.

Listed in the following sections, however, are some of the more important bibliographies and other reference sources relevant to political science, classified roughly into segments or sub-fields of the discipline. General, non-reference books are not included; the student will be exposed to these in his courses, and they will be listed in various bibliographies. Even with this major omission, the listing is highly selective. Only English-language sources are covered. Many specialized sources have been omitted deliberately, and some important works may have been overlooked. In other words, the usual *mea culpa* which authors are supposed to make is in effect.

Chapter 11

General Political
Science Sources

Political science has become so specialized, and its literature so voluminous, that it is impossible—except in a highly selective
manner—to cover the whole discipline in bibliographies and other
reference sources. As a result, general sources tend to resemble the
basic introductory course in political science, in which the instructor conducts students on a fast tour around the top of the
iceberg, pointing all the while to the great mass below the waterline,
which they will explore later in advanced courses. Nevertheless,
there are several general sources of considerable utility.

GUIDES TO READING AND REFERENCE MATERIALS

Hoselitz, Bert F., ed. *A Reader's Guide to the Social Sciences*. Glencoe,
Ill.: Free Press, 1959. A collection of essays on the various social
science disciplines. Chapter 4 on "Political Science," by Heinz Eulau
is an excellent brief review and critique of the landmark works in
the field. The graduate student facing orals and who feels weak on
"bibliography" will find it well worthwhile. Eulau's essay is now dated,
but may be supplemented to some extent by:

Connery, Robert H., et al. *Reading Guide in Politics and Government*.
Washington: National Council for the Social Studies, 1966. (Bulletin
No. 38.) An annotated list of important books on American and foreign
government and politics. Designed primarily for the high school gov-

ernment teacher, but a very useful review for the political science major.

Political Science Annual; an international review. Indianapolis: Bobbs-Merrill, Vol. 1. 1966–   . Designed to "contribute periodic inventories of selected aspects of political science." Each annual volume will contain a few critical reviews of the state of research in various segments of political science. Volume 1 has long reviews on "Political Socialization" by Richard Dawson, on "Legislative Institutions and Processes" by Heinz Eulau and Katherine Hinckley, on "Public Opinion and Opinion Change" by Bernard Hennessy, and on "An Application of the Policy Science Orientation; the sharing of power in a psychiatric hospital," by Harold Lasswell and Robert Rubenstein. Each article has a bibliography of relevant literature.

MacKenzie, Norman, ed. *A Guide to the Social Sciences.* New York: New American Lib., 1966. A collection of essays designed to introduce the non-specialist to the social sciences. There is a chapter by Jean Blondel on "Government" and a chapter by James McGregor Burns on "Political Ideology."

Harmon, Robert B. *Political Science; a bibliographical guide to the literature.* Metuchen, N.J.: Scarecrow Press, 1965. The most extensive recent bibliography in the field, listing both reference and general books, though mostly without annotations. Has sections on Comparative Government, State and Local Government, Political Parties, Public Opinion and Electoral Processes; Political Theory; Law and Jurisprudence; Public Administration; and International Relations. Appendix A contains a selected list of major political science periodicals and indicates where they are indexed. Updated by Harmon's *Political Science; a bibliographical guide to the literature; supplement 1968.* Metuchen, N.J.: Scarecrow Press, 1968.

Wynar, Lubomyr R. *Guide to Reference Materials in Political Science; a selective bibliography.* 2 vols. Denver: Libraries Unlimited, Inc., Colorado Bibliographic Inst., 1968. Similar to Harmon, combining general and reference materials, but with somewhat more emphasis on reference sources. Only the major works are annotated. Volume I has sections on "Social Science General Reference Sources" (which supplements the White volume listed below), "Political Science General Reference Sources," "Political Theory" and "Ideology." Volume II covers "International Relations," "Public Administration," "Political

Behavior," "Comparative Political Systems," "Government Documents" and "Reference Sources in Law."

Pogany, Andras H. and Hortenzia L. *Political Science and International Relations; books recommended for the use of American Catholic college and university libraries.* Metuchen, N.J.: Scarecrow Press, 1967. An unannotated list of over 5,800 books published between 1955 and 1966. Intended as a book selection guide for Catholic libraries.

White, Carl M., ed. *Sources of Information in the Social Sciences; a guide to the literature.* Totowa, N.J.: Bedminster Press, 1964. A well-selected and organized guide to the general and reference literatures of "History," "Economics and Business Administration," "Sociology," "Anthropology," "Psychology" and "Education." Chapter 8, on "Political Science," has an introductory section by Heinz Eulau which summarizes the state of the art in various sub-fields and lists 242 major substantive works in these sub-fields. Following this is an annotated listing of 161 bibliographies and other reference tools.

Clarke, Jack A. *Research Materials in the Social Sciences.* 2nd ed. Madison: Univ. of Wisconsin Press, 1967. An annotated bibliography of 215 major reference tools in various social science fields. Too brief to be of much use to the political science student in his own field, but will supplement White and Wynar as an introduction to reference sources in other disciplines.

Mason, John Brown, ed. *Research Resources: annotated guides to the social sciences.* Santa Barbara, Calif.: American Bibliographical Center-Clio Press, 1968. Volume I, entitled "International Relations and Recent History," lists and describes periodicals, reference books, indexes and other sources on international relations and current affairs. Volume II, published in 1969, covers official publications of the U.S. government, the United Nations, and other international organizations.

Lewis, Peter R. *The Literature of the Social Sciences; an introductory survey and guide.* London: The Library Assn., 1960. Similar to White and Clarke, though much more selective than White. Chapter 7 is on "Political Science," with some emphasis on British sources.

Burchfield, Laverne. *Student's Guide to Materials in Political Science.* New York: Holt, 1935. An excellent work in its time, produced under the auspices of the American Political Science Association. Covered all of the sub-fields of the discipline and listed periodical articles as well as general books and reference sources. Since 1935 the literature of political science has expanded far too much to allow for a similarly comprehensive work today. Unfortunately, Burchfield is so far out-of-date as to be of little use to the contemporary student.

As will be obvious, this guide is similar to several of the others listed above. In some respects, they are the competition. Faced with such a variety of sources, the student is entitled to some (hopefully objective) advice. This guide, I think, has two advantages over the others listed: (1) None of the others contains the explanatory, "how-to-do-it-on-your-own" information contained in Part A above; (2) Part B should largely supersede the others in so far as the coverage of bibliographies and other reference sources in political science is concerned.

On the other hand, this guide has two disadvantages or gaps in coverage. It does not attempt to cover reference materials in other disciplines, except briefly in the listing of "Indexes and Abstracts in Other Disciplines" in Chapter 3. For this type of coverage the student should consult White, the section in Wynar on "Social Science General Reference Sources," and (for briefer treatment) Clarke and Lewis. Second, it does not list general, non-reference books in political science. As indicated earlier, the student will be exposed to these as part of his courses. Those who need help in this area, however, should consult Harmon, Wynar or Pogany (for listings of books) and White or Hoselitz (for a selection and critical analysis of major works).

BIBLIOGRAPHIES

The guides listed above place more emphasis upon reference works than upon general books and monographs. No one bibliography provides really adequate or current coverage of the thousands of books on political science subjects which are published. The *International Bibliography of Political Science,* which is both a periodical index and a bibliography of books, comes closest and is described in Chapter 3 of this guide. The items listed below either deal with the social sciences in general or, where they cover only political science, are highly selective.

London Bibliography of the Social Sciences. London: London Sch. of Economics, 1931– . The most extensive bibliography of books, pamphlets, and other monographic works in the social sciences. Lists, by subject, the holdings of several London libraries, including the British Library of Political and Economic Science. Thirteen volumes have been published to date, listing works added to the libraries up to 1962.

U.S. Library of Congress. *Library of Congress Catalog. Books: Subjects*. Washington: Card Division, Lib. of Congress, 1950– . A subject listing of books, published since 1945, which have been cataloged by the Library of Congress and other major libraries. Issued quarterly, with annual cumulations. The *National Union Catalog,* also issued by the Library of Congress, provides a listing of books by author and indicates libraries where they are located.

Harvard Univ. Library. *Government*. (Widener Library Shelflist, No. 21). Cambridge: Harvard Univ. Press, 1969. A computer-produced listing of books on government and politics in the Harvard Library. Arranged by the classification system used by the Widener Library, with author and title indexes. No annotations, but probably the most extensive single booklist available.

Burdette, Franklin. *Political Science; a selected bibliography of books in print*. College Park: Bureau of Governmental Research, Univ. of Maryland, 1961. "Brief annotated bibliography of significant books in print in the major fields of political science." Highly selective (approximately 250 authors) and now somewhat dated, but a good basic listing.

Holland, Henry M. *A Checklist of Paperback Books and Reprints in Political Science*. Washington: American Political Science Assn., 1962. A brief listing of the most important political science books available in paperback. Can be updated by using *Paperbound Books in Print,* published by the R. R. Bowker Co. of New York, issued monthly and cumulated three times a year. This has separate sections on Government and Politics, Law, and World Affairs.

Quarterly Check-List of Economics and Political Science. Darien, Conn.: American Bibliographic Service, 1958– . An unannotated listing of recently published books, arranged by author.

United Nations Educational, Scientific, and Cultural Organization. *World List of Social Science Periodicals*. 3rd ed. Paris: UNESCO, 1966. A list, by country with a subject index, of scholarly journals in the social sciences. Brief descriptions indicate type of articles carried by each journal and the extent of its book reviewing. May be updated through the listing of new social science periodicals in the quarterly *Social Science Information,* published by the International Social Science Council.

Katz, Bill, ed. *Magazines for Libraries; for the general reader and for public, school, junior college and college libraries.* New York: R. R. Bowker, 1969. A selective guide to magazines, which contains large sections on "Political Science," "Sociology" and "Literary and Political Reviews." Each magazine selected is described in detail, and students will find it particularly useful for the balance it maintains between highly scholarly journals and more general publications.

BIBLIOGRAPHIES OF DISSERTATIONS AND THESES

For most purposes, most students will not find it necessary to go beyond published works in their literature searching. If he really wants to exhaust a subject, however, or be sure that he is aware of the latest research in his field, the student may need to search for unpublished dissertations and theses done at other universities. For advanced students who are beginning work on their own dissertations and theses, such searching usually is required. Though the actual acquisition of dissertation and theses may be time-consuming, and perhaps expensive, there are several sources to check.

"Doctoral Dissertations in Political Science in Universities of the United States and Canada"—This list is published annually in the September issue of the *American Political Science Review,* with one section on "Dissertations in Progress" and another on "Dissertations Completed Since the Last Listing." The listing is by broad subjects such as Political Philosophy, American State and Local Government, Public Administration, etc. The author, title, and university are given, but no abstract or annotation indicating contents.

Dissertation Abstracts. Ann Arbor, Mich.: University Microfilms, 1952– . A monthly compilation of abstracts of doctoral dissertations completed in about 160 universities. Covers all subject fields, but has a section on "Political Science" with sub-sections on "International Law and Relations" and "Public Administration." For each dissertation listed, there is a 300–400 word abstract prepared by the author.

The dissertations themselves may be purchased from University Microfilms, either in Xerox copy or microfilm; prices and ordering information are given. Each issue of *Dissertation Abstracts* has a subject and author index which is cumulated annually. University Microfilms also publishes an *Index to American Doctoral Dissertations* (issued annually as no. 13 of *Dissertation Abstracts*), which is a consolidated list of dissertations for which doctoral degrees were awarded during the previous academic year. This includes some dissertations which did not appear in *Dissertation Abstracts*. Recently University Microfilms announced a new computer-based search service, called "DATRIX," through which an individual can request a "keyword" search of all dissertations listed in *Dissertation Abstracts;* see the introductory pages of any recent issue of *Dissertation Abstracts* for details and costs.

Masters Abstracts; a catalog of selected masters theses on microfilm. Ann Arbor, Mich.: University Microfilms, 1962–   . A highly selective listing of masters theses, with abstracts, available from University Microfilms. Issued quarterly, with a cumulative subject and author index beginning with Volume VI, 1968. So far only a few universities are participating in this program, and less than a hundred political science theses are listed each year.

OTHER REFERENCE SOURCES

Sills, David, ed. *International Encyclopedia of the Social Sciences*. 15 vs. New York: Macmillan and the Free Press, 1968. This long-awaited opus supplements the old *Encyclopedia of the Social Sciences,* published in the early 1930's. The work in effect is a much-needed synthesis and summary of the "state of the art" in all the social sciences. Consisting of original articles contributed by leading social scientists, it covers the disciplines of Anthropology, Economics, Geography, History, Law, Political Science, Psychiatry, Psychology, Sociology, and Statistics. Reflecting trends in the social sciences since the earlier encyclopedia, the emphasis is upon analytic and comparative aspects of a subject, with historical and descriptive material included chiefly to illustrate concepts and theories. Well-selected bibliographies follow the articles, which are arranged alphabetically with numerous cross references and a detailed index in a separate volume.

There are over 180 articles dealing directly with political science subjects, with many other articles covering related topics. Most of the major articles run from eight to twelve pages and provide expert, concise coverage; Easton on "Political Science," Eulau on "Political Behavior," Janowitz on "Political Sociology," Schubert on "Judicial Behavior," Stokes on "Voting," etc.

The encyclopedia should serve several functions for political science students. For the undergraduate, it offers a brief, relatively simple introduction into the mysteries of a new field. When his instructor starts to talk about systems analysis, he can read William Mitchell on "Political Systems" and get safely through the first few weeks. The articles on other social science fields may serve somewhat the same function for the graduate student. And for awhile at least, the political science articles will provide him with a nice, neat review package in those mind-blowing days just before comprehensive exams.

Public Policy; a yearbook of the Graduate School of Public Administration, Harvard University. Cambridge: Harvard Univ. Press, 1940– . Each volume contains several essays on various political science subjects; not limited to public administration only. The 1966 volume, for example, has 15 essays under the topic headings of Domestic Issues, Foreign Policy, and Problems of Development.

Facts on File; world news digest with index. New York: Facts on File, 1940– . A weekly, loose-leaf news digest with sections on "World Affairs," "National Affairs," etc. Indexes are published weekly and cumulated through a year, with five-year cumulated indexes. Sources are not identified. Not the kind of thing you would cite in a scholarly paper, but useful for verifying dates, events, etc., and as a capsule summary of the news.

Keesing's Contemporary Archives; weekly diary of world events. London: Keesing's 1931– . A British news digest similar to *Facts on File,* but with more extensive documentation and coverage of foreign news. Frequently carries the full text of important speeches by world leaders or official government pronouncements. Sources are identified. Subject and names indexes cumulated frequently.

Back, Harry, et al. *Polec; dictionary of politics and economics.* 2nd ed. Berlin: Walter de Gruyter, 1967. There are several dictionaries of political science, most of them tending to emphasize historical or traditional definitions or concepts. This combination English-French-German dictionary is one of the better recent works. A standard American work is *White's Political Dictionary* (New York: World, 1947). Joseph Dunner's *Dictionary of Political Science* (New York: Philosophical Library, 1964) is the most up-to-date general dictionary in the field.

Cranston, Maurice, ed. *A Glossary of Political Terms.* London: The Bodley Head, 1966. Brief two- or three-page essays on about 40 concepts or doctrines encountered in discussions of political problems.

Safire, William. *The New Language of Politics; an anecdotal dictionary of catchwords, slogans and political usage.* New York: Random House, 1968. Explains derivation and history of words, terms, and phrases by and about politicians. Not an academic-type dictionary. "This is a dictionary of the words and phrases that have misled millions, blackened reputations, held out false hopes, oversimplified ideas to appeal to the lowest common denominator, shouted down inquiry, and replaced searching debate with stereotypes that trigger approval or hatred."

Theimer, Walter. *An Encyclopedia of Modern World Politics.* New York: Rinehart, 1950. A survey of "political terms, systems, treaties, problems, and watchwords of the contemporary world." Now dated, but still of some use.

Biographical Directory of the American Political Science Association. 5th ed. Washington: American Political Science Assn., 1968. Contains brief biographical sketches of approximately 12,000 members of the APSA. Appendices contain a classification of members by fields of interest and by locale.

Political Handbook and Atlas of the World; parliaments, parties, and press. New York: Council on Foreign Relations, 1927– . Lists leading government and party officials, gives composition of parliaments, and lists leading newspapers for each country, with their political affiliation. The latter information is by self-designation and is not to be taken seriously in all cases, e.g., the *Indianapolis News,* edited by M. Stanton Evans, is listed as "Independent."

U.S. Library of Congress. National Referral Center for Science and Technology. *A Directory of Information Resources in the United States: Social Sciences.* Washington: Govt. Printing Off., 1965. An alphabetical listing of public and private organizations, institutes, research agencies, libraries, etc., which contain significant information resources in the social sciences. Brief description of each, with a list of publications. Subject index indicates those resources relating to political science.

Statesman's Yearbook; statistical and historical annual of the states of the world. London: The Macmillan Company, 1864– . An annual containing concise descriptive and statistical information on all countries. Each country summary has sections on government, constitutional structure, finances, defense and foreign affairs, lists of principal officials, and a bibliography of selected reference books and statistical compendia. The oldest and most authoritative of the general yearbooks.

International Yearbook and Statesmen's Who's Who. London: Burke's Peerage Ltd., 1953– . Similar to *Statesman's Yearbook,* with brief information on each country. Has a separate "Biographical Section" containing sketches on about 8,000 leading world figures in government, business, education and other fields.

Almanac of Current World Leaders. Los Angeles: Llewellyn Pubns., 1958– . Designed "to keep students, teachers and librarians with as current as possible single reference source of governmental changes among the world's governments." For each country, lists leading officials down through the cabinet level. Indicates each nation's memberships in international organizations. Published three times a year with monthly supplements between issues.

Europa Yearbook. London: Europa Publications Ltd., 1959– . Volume I covers International Organizations and Europe, Volume II covers Africa, The Americas, Asia and Australasia. Same type of information as in other yearbooks, but with somewhat more emphasis on government. Has a section on "Diplomatic Representation" which lists embassies and legations accredited to each country. A companion volume, entitled *The Middle East and North Africa,* contains more detailed information on countries in these areas.

Worldmark Encyclopedia of the Nations. 3rd ed. New York: Harper & Row, 1965. "A practical guide to the geographic, historical, political, social and economic status of all nations, their international relationships, and the United Nations system." Consists of five volumes on various regions. The first volume has a summary of the United Nations and other inter-governmental organizations, with a table showing member countries.

Other yearbooks, directories, news digests, etc., which focus on specific regions or countries are described below in the chapter on "Comparative Politics and Area Studies."

Chapter **12**

American
Government
and Politics

Librarians sometimes suspect that there is an "inverse law of bibliography" in effect, according to which "the greater the mass of material published on a subject, the less bibliographical apparatus there is to support it." Such a tendency, at least, appears to be operating in the subject area of American government and politics. There are virtually no general bibliographies covering this very broad sub-field of political science; most of the bibliographies listed below are specialized, focusing on some fairly narrow segment of the subject. Generally, this is an area where the student may need to rely heavily upon bibliographies appended to books, upon bibliographical articles, or upon the indexes and abstracts discussed in Chapter 3.

GUIDES TO READING AND RESEARCH

Schattschneider, E. E., et al. *A Guide to the Study of Public Affairs.* New York: Dryden Press, 1952. A useful introduction, particularly for the beginning student. Has chapters on "How to Study a Pressure Group," "How to Study a Federal Government Agency or Department," "How to Study the Record of a Member of Congress," etc.

Tompkins, Dorothy C. *Materials for the Study of Federal Government.* Chicago: Public Admin. Service, 1948. Now dated but still of some value for its discussion of government publications relevant to political science.

U.S. Library of Congress. *A Guide to the Study of the United States of America.* Washington: Govt. Printing Off., 1960. An extensive listing of "representative books reflecting the development of American life and thought." Has a heavy historical emphasis, but chapters on Constitution and Government; Politics, Parties, and Elections; Diplomatic History and Foreign Relations will be useful, particularly for the annotations of important books. A revised edition is in preparation.

BIBLIOGRAPHIES

Jones, Charles O. and Randall B. Ripley. *Role of Political Parties in Congress; a bibliography and research guide.* Tucson: Univ. of Arizona Press, 1966. A bibliography of books and articles, with sections on General Works, Congressional Organization and Procedure, Party Organization and Procedure, Party Leadership, Party Voting and Methodology, Congressional Elections, Constituency and Congress.

The Legislative Process; a bibliography in legislative behavior. East Lansing: Inst. for Community Development and Services, Michigan State Univ., 1963. An unannotated list of about 400 articles and books analyzing American national and state legislative behavior.

Jonas, Frank H., ed. *Bibliography on Western Politics; selected, annotated, with introductory essays.* Published as a supplement to the *Western Political Quarterly* for December, 1958. "Undertakes to collect and classify the source materials of special significance in Western politics." One section on Western politics in general, with separate sections on each of eleven Western states.

Bachelder, Glen L. and Paul C. Shaw. *Literature of Federalism; a selected bibliography.* rev. ed. East Lansing: Inst. for Community Development and Studies, Michigan State Univ., 1966. A brief, unannotated list of books and articles on federalism in the U.S. and other countries.

Brooks, Alexander D. *Civil Rights and Liberties in the United States; an annotated bibliography.* New York: Civil Liberties Educational Foundation, 1962. A classified bibliography of about 1,500 books and audio-visual materials, published since 1940, on civil rights, civil liberties, intergroup relations, discrimination and related subjects.

McCoy, Ralph E. *Freedom of the Press; an annotated bibliography.* Carbondale: Southern Illinois Univ. Press, 1968. A descriptive bibliography of over 8,000 books, articles, and other writings on freedom of the press in English-speaking countries. Arranged alphabetically with subject index. Provides both historical and current coverage and is the most extensive bibliography available on freedom of the press.

Mugridge, Donald H. *The Presidents of the United States, 1789–1962; a selected list of references.* Washington: Lib. of Congress, 1963. An annotated bibliography of writings by and biographies of each President, with preliminary sections listing writings on The Presidency, Presidential Elections, and the Vice-Presidency. The number of biographies range from 141 on Lincoln down to two on Millard Fillmore.

Tompkins, Dorothy C. *Presidential Succession; a bibliography.* Berkeley: Inst. of Governmental Studies, Univ. of California, 1965. Brief bibliography of about 100 recent articles, books, and documents on the problems of Presidential disability and succession.

Tompkins, Dorothy C. *Changes in Congress; proposals to change Congress—terms of members of the House; a bibliography.* Berkeley, Calif.: Inst. of Governmental Studies, Univ. of California, 1966. An unannotated bibliography of about 200 books, articles, and official documents on criticism of and proposals to change Congress since the Legislative Reorganization Act of 1946.

Caldwell, Lynton K., ed. *Science, Technology, and Public Policy; a selected and annotated bibliography.* 2 vols. Bloomington: Department of Govt., Indiana Univ., 1968. A bibliography, with extensive annotations, of about 5,000 writings which "focus upon public affairs and public policies in relation to science and technology." Lists material published from 1945 to the end of 1967. Volume I covers books, monographs, government documents and whole issues of periodicals; Volume II lists periodical articles. Though not limited to American experience, the emphasis is upon U.S. public policy as it relates to science and technology. Items are classified into twelve subject areas; section five on "Science, Politics, and Government" probably will be the most relevant for political scientists.

Law and Society Review. Beverly Hills, Calif.: Sage Pubns., 1966–   .
The *Review* publishes substantive articles "by lawyers, social scientists,
and other scholars which bear on the relationship between law and the
social sciences." Each quarterly issue also carries a selected bibliography of books and articles which includes sections on "Judicial
Process and Behavior" and "Civil Liberties, Civil Rights, and Race
Relations."

Tompkins, Dorothy C. *The Supreme Court of the United States; a bibliography*. Berkeley: Bureau of Public Admin., Univ. of California,
1959. A bibliography of about 1,500 writings, generally unannotated,
on the organization and work of the Court, its membership and relations to other branches of government.

Klein, Fannie J. *Judicial Administration and the Legal Profession; a bibliography*. Dobbs Ferry, N.Y.: Oceana Pubns., 1963. Lists over 6,600
books and articles, with a heavy legal emphasis, but of some political
science interest.

Tompkins, Dorothy C. *Conflict of Interest in the Federal Government; a
bibliography*. Berkeley: Bureau of Public Admin., Univ. of California,
1961. Lists primarily government publications, with emphasis on the
years since 1950.

Television in Government and Politics; a bibliography. New York: Television Information Off., 1964. List of popular and scholarly writing on
relationships between television and politics.

Muller, Robert H., ed. *From Radical Left to Extreme Right; current
periodicals of protest, controversy, or dissent-U.S.A.* Ann Arbor,
Mich.: Campus Publishers, 1967. "A bibliography containing dis-
passionate summaries of content samples to guide librarians and other
educators through the polemic fringe." Lists, describes, and analyzes
content of 163 periodicals, giving addresses and circulation, if known.

Goldwater, Walter. *Radical Periodicals in America, 1890–1950; a bibliography with brief notes*. New Haven: Yale Univ. Library, 1964. An
annotated bibliography of 321 periodicals "published in the United
States, in the English language, of a 'radical'—i.e., Anarchist, Communist, or Socialist—nature, between 1890 and 1950."

Fuerst, Martin J. *Bibliography on the Origins and History of the John Birch Society.* 5th ed. The St. Didacus Press, 1965. An unannotated listing of over 2,000 references to the Birch Society in books, periodicals, and newspaper articles.

OTHER REFERENCE SOURCES

Congressional Quarterly Weekly Report. Washington: Congressional Quarterly Service, 1943– . An objective summary and analysis of events in Congress and the federal government generally. Each issue has sections analyzing the status of legislation in committee and on the floor of Congress, with roll-call votes. Noted for its coverage of lobby spending. Though the emphasis is on Congress, it also covers major developments within executive departments and the judiciary. An Index to the *Weekly Report* is issued quarterly and cumulated annually. CQ also publishes an annual volume entitled *Congressional Quarterly Almanac* which pulls together much of the material appearing in the weekly reports. The *Almanac* does not completely supersede the *Weekly Report,* however, as the latter will contain much detail not reproduced in the annual volume. In recent years CQ has begun publishing a series of "Special Reports" on the national elections, civil rights and other topics.

Congress and the Nation, 1945–1964; a review of government and politics in the postwar years. Washington: Congressional Quarterly Service, 1965. An encyclopedic (over 1,700 pages) survey, summarizing Congressional legislation and political activity during these years. A distillation and elaboration of information contained in the annual *CQ Almanac* for this 20-year period. Purpose is "to provide essential details in the fields of legislation and politics from 1945 to 1964." Part I on "Review of Legislation and Politics" has seventeen chapters on Foreign Policy, Civil Rights, Lobbies, Federal-State Relations and other topics. Each chapter has a concise review of legislative activity on the subject, plus a summary of the existing state of legislation as of 1964. Part II, a "Directory of Persons and Events" which lists Cabinet officials and other government officers during this period, includes a record of key votes in Congress and a summary of major Supreme Court decisions. The best starting point for study of Congressional legislation during these years; for information in greater depth, the student can go from this source to the annual *CQ Almanac* and the *Weekly Reports.*

CQ Guide to Current American Government. Washington: Congressional Quarterly Service, 1963– . Issued twice a year as an "up-to-date handbook for the study of American government." Contains material which appears in the *Congressional Quarterly Weekly Report,* "rearranged and rewritten for classes and study use." Has sections on the Presidency, Congress, Politics, and the Federal Judiciary.

American Government Annual. New York: Holt, Rinehart & Winston, 1958/59– . Each volume contains five or six essays by political scientists on various current topics in American government and politics. Designed to provide "current and analytical materials to help students, particularly in American government, relate what they read in newspapers and see happening about them to their classroom experiences." Each volume contains a brief "List of Suggested Readings."

Issues; documents in current American government and politics. New York: Crowell, 1965/66– . Reproduces important documents or statements by political leaders or academic specialists on current affairs. Designed to supplement materials usually assigned in the basic course on American government.

United States Government Organization Manual. Washington: Govt. Printing Off., 1935– . The "official organization handbook of the Federal Government," published annually. Has descriptive sections on all government agencies, including statement of purpose or authority and lists of key officials. Includes organization charts and appendices listing abolished or transferred agencies and the major publications of the various agencies.

Official Congressional Directory. Washington: Govt. Printing Off., 1809– . Contains biographical sketches of Congressmen, their committee assignments, list of foreign diplomatic representatives in the U.S., directory of members of the press accredited to Congress, and much other information. The "Alphabetical List of Members of Congress" gives their Washington address and has symbols indicating those Congressmen who are married, those having unmarried daughters, and "those having other ladies with them" (?!).

Congressional Staff Directory. Comp. and ed. by Charles B. Brownson. Washington: Congressional Staff Directory, 1961– . A private publication similar to the *Official Congressional Directory,* but with emphasis on biographical sketches and assignments of Congressional staff members. Also has a "List of Representatives by Major Cities."

U.S. Bureau of the Census. *Congressional District Atlas (Districts of the 91st Congress).* Washington: Govt. Printing Off., 1968. Presents maps showing the boundaries of Congressional districts, with detailed maps for metropolitan districts plus lists showing district location of counties and larger cities. The maps in this new edition show all redistricting actions up to August 1, 1968.

U.S. Congress. *Biographical Directory of the American Congress, 1774–1961.* Washington: Govt. Printing Off., 1961. Biographical sketches of all persons who have served in Congress, plus a listing of members of each Congress. Also has a list of Executive officers, 1789–1961.

Since 1951 the *Western Political Quarterly* has carried a series of annual articles by Floyd M. Riddick, Parliamentarian of the U.S. Senate, which summarize the activity of each Congressional session, with an emphasis on procedural matters.

Federal Register. Washington: Govt. Printing Off., 1936– . A daily compilation of executive orders, administrative regulations and rules, and a mass of regulatory decrees emanating from executive agencies, commissions, etc. Has monthly, quarterly and annual indexes which are cumulative. Roughly the equivalent of the *Congressional Record* for executive agencies. For details on its format and how to use it, see Chapter 11 of Laurence F. Schmeckebier and Roy B. Eastin, *Government Publications and Their Use.* rev. ed. Washington: Brookings Institution, 1961.

U.S. National Archives and Records Service. *Weekly Compilation of Presidential Documents,* August 2, 1965– . Washington: Govt. Printing Off., 1965– . Despite the world's most massive publishing operation, only recently has the U.S. government seen to it that the pronouncements of its chief executive officer saw the light of print. This compilation contains transcripts of the President's news conferences, messages to Congress, public speeches and other statements, plus other Presidential pronouncements. A weekly index, which is cumulated quarterly and annually, allows quick subject access to the material included.

U.S. National Archives and Records Service. *Public Papers of the Presidents of the United States*. Washington: Govt. Printing Off., 1958– .
Beginning with Eisenhower in 1957, the National Archives began publishing an annual volume containing the public papers and statements of the President. Since then the series has been carried back to the beginning of Truman's administration in 1945 and through Johnson for 1967. It will be continued, and apparently each volume will pull together the material published weekly in the compilation referred to above. For a discussion of the availability of Presidential papers prior to 1945, see Chapter 12 of Schmeckebier and Eastin.

Small, Norman J., ed. *The Constitution of the United States of America; analysis and interpretation*. 1964 ed. Washington: Govt. Printing Off., 1964. (Senate Document 39, 88th Congress, 1st Session.) A detailed article-by-article and section-by-section analysis of the Constitution, referring to and analyzing Supreme Court decisions bearing on its interpretation. Similarly detailed coverage of each amendment to the Constitution. Appendices list the several hundred federal and state acts and municipal ordinances held to be unconstitutional by the Supreme Court. Has a subject index and alphabetical Table of Cases. The 1964 edition is an updating and revision of the classic 1952 edition by Edward S. Corwin.

The Supreme Court Review. Chicago: Univ. of Chicago Press, 1960– .
Each annual volume contains five or six essays on particular cases, types of cases, or trends within the Supreme Court. Designed to provide a forum "in which the best minds in the field will be encouraged to express their critical judgment" of the Court's work.

Emerson, Thomas I., et al. *Political and Civil Rights in the United States*. 3rd ed. Boston: Little, Brown, 1967. Aim is "to present, primarily from the legal point of view, some of the basic materials . . . concerning the fundamental rights of the individual in modern society." Contains texts of important documents, court decisions, and other materials on freedom of expression, freedom of religion, discrimination, and related subjects.

Porter, Kirk H. and Donald Johnson. *National Party Platforms, 1840–1964*. 3rd ed. Urbana: Univ. of Illinois Press, 1966. Contains texts of all major and minor party platforms for these years.

National Municipal League. *Presidential Nominating Procedures in 1964; a state-by-state report*. New York: National Municipal League, 1965. Contains responses by specialists in each state to eleven questions regarding party nominating practices and procedures. Responses are cumulated into an overall national summary. Updates information in *Presidential Nominating Politics in 1952*, published by the Brookings Institution.

Theis, Paul A. and Edmund L. Henshaw. *Who's Who in American Politics; a biographical directory of United States political leaders*. 1st ed., 1967–1968. New York: R. R. Bowker, 1967. Contains biographical sketches of 12,500 individuals active in American politics. Gives education, political position, group memberships and other information. Most useful for its coverage of local political and governmental figures.

Plano, Jack C. and Milton Greenberg. *The American Political Dictionary*. 2nd ed. New York: Holt, Rinehart & Winston, 1967. Covers over a thousand "terms, agencies, court cases, and statutes which are considered to be the most relevant for a basic comprehension of American government institutions, practices, and problems."

Sperber, Hans and Travis Trittschuh. *American Political Terms; an historical dictionary*. Detroit: Wayne State Univ. Press, 1962. Wider, but briefer, coverage than Plano and Greenberg, with heavy historical emphasis.

Smith, Edward C. and Arnold J. Zurcher. *Dictionary of American Politics*. 2nd ed. New York: Barnes & Noble, 1968. A standard work, recently revised, containing brief definitions of over 3,800 terms.

First National Directory of "Rightist" Groups, Publications, and Some Individuals. 5th ed. Los Angeles: Alert Americans Assn., 1965. A listing of over 2,000 right-wing or conservative groups, etc., giving addresses. Compiled by a self-designated rightist group, which does not guarantee the accuracy of the listings.

Group Research, Inc. *Directory*. Washington: Group Research, 1962. A directory of organizations, individuals, and publications, designed as a "ready reference on groups attempting to influence governmental and economic affairs." For organizations, gives brief history, statement of purpose or policy, list of officers, and publications, and some financial data. The emphasis is upon right-wing groups. Has a section of "Special Reports" which contains longer analyses of particular groups or topics, such as one on "Finances of the Right Wing." The basic directory was started in 1962 and has since been supplemented on a periodic basis. According to the *Congressional Quarterly Weekly Report,* Group Research, Inc., was "founded in 1962 to report on right wing activities and headed by Wesley McCune, former newspaperman, Agriculture Department official and publicity man for the Democratic National Committee."

RATINGS OF CONGRESSIONAL VOTING RECORDS

Several interest groups publish evaluations of the voting records of individual senators and representatives. Typically, these consist of a selection of ten to fifteen roll-call votes for each session of Congress, along with a "rating" indicating whether a legislator voted "right" or "wrong" from the group's point of view. The Americans for Democratic Action (ADA) has published such ratings each year since 1947, usually in the September or October issue of its newspaper, *ADA World.* ADA's conservative counterpart, the Americans for Constitutional Action (ACA), began publishing its *ACA-Index* in 1960. Ratings by other groups, such as the American Farm Bureau Federation (AFBA), National Farmers Union (NFU), the AFL-CIO Committee on Political Education (COPE) and the Chamber of Commerce of the U.S., have appeared sporadically in the official publications of these organizations. Many of these publications are rather fugitive and may not be available in most libraries. Since 1960, however, the *Congressional Quarterly Weekly Report* has gathered, summarized, and published ratings made by the major groups. The following issues of the *Weekly Report* contain ratings for the Congresses and groups indicated:

October 7, 1960—86th Congress; ratings of: ACA, ADA, AFBF, COPE, NFU, and Civic Affairs Associates.

October 26, 1962—87th Congress; ratings of: ACA, ADA, AFBF, COPE, NFU, and Civic Affairs Associates.

October 23, 1964—88th Congress; ratings of: ACA, ADA, AFBF, COPE, NFU, and National Associated Businessmen.

February 25, 1966—89th Congress, 1st Session; ratings of: ACA, ADA, AFBF, Chamber of Commerce, NFU.

November 4, 1966—89th Congress, 2nd Session; ratings of: ACA, ADA, COPE, and National Associated Businessmen.

April 26, 1968—90th Congress, 1st Session; ratings of: ACA, ADA, COPE, and Chamber of Commerce.

November 22, 1968—90th Congress, 2nd Session; ratings of: ACA, ADA, COPE, and National Associated Businessmen.

Chapter 13

Political Behavior
and Public Opinion

These areas of political science are the least library-oriented of any segments of the discipline. While the library may still be the laboratory of the political philosopher and other document-oriented specialists, the laboratory of the behavioralists, as their coda specifies, is man. In their largely successful efforts to reorient the discipline, some behavioralists have urged political scientists to "get out of the library and into the field." As a result of the newness of behavioral work, and perhaps partly as a result of the negative reaction to the earlier preoccupation of political science with documentary sources, there is today relatively little in the library of interest to behavioralists.

On the other hand, few libraries have made the adjustments which behavioral work requires, since they have not made room for tapes, card decks, and the computers to process them. Even so, in the bibliographic sense at least, there are some library materials relevant to behavioral work.

BIBLIOGRAPHIES

U.S. Department of State. Bureau of Intelligence and Research. *Political Behavior; a list of current studies.* Washington: Department of State, 1963. Lists studies recently completed or currently in progress on all aspects of political behavior. Annotations indicate scope of each study and methodology employed.

Bendix, Reinhard and Seymour M. Lipset. "Political Sociology; an essay with special reference to the development of research in the United States and Western Europe," *Current Sociology,* Vol. VI, No. 2, 1957. An analytical essay plus annotated bibliography of over 800 books and articles, with sections on Political Parties, Public Opinion, Pressure Groups, Voting Behavior, etc. Can be updated by using *Sociological Abstracts,* which is detailed in Chapter 3.

Mayntz, Renate. "The Study of Organizations; a trend report and bibliography," *Current Sociology,* Vol. XIII, No. 3, 1965. Analyzes writings on "formal, complex, or large-scale organizations," with annotated bibliography of over 500 articles and books. Has sections on Administrative Organizations and Voluntary Associations.

Eisenstadt, S. N. "Bureaucracy and Bureaucratization; a trend report and bibliography," *Current Sociology,* Vol. VII, No. 2, 1958. Contains a long article analyzing trends in bureaucracies, plus an annotated bibliography of over 600 books and articles.

Beck, Carl and Thomas McKechnie. *Political Elites; a select computerized bibliography.* Cambridge, Mass.: M.I.T. Press, 1968. A bibliography of about 4,000 books and articles containing information relevant to the study of political elites in all areas. Section I is a "Keyword Title Listing" of the literature. Section II contains full citations to the items listed in the first section, plus a code indicating the relevance of the item to seven general topics of elite studies: "General Elite Theory," "Composition of Elites," etc. Section III is an author list. Produced as a by-product of the substantive studies of elites at M.I.T.

Wasserman, Paul. *Decision-making; an annotated bibliography.* Ithaca, N.Y.: Grad. Sch. of Business and Public Admin., Cornell Univ., 1958. Well-selected bibliography of major books and articles, and not limited to business decision-making. A *Supplement* has been issued covering the period 1958–1963.

Albert, Ethel and Clyde Kluckhohn. *A Selected Bibliography on Values, Ethics, and Esthetics in the Behavioral Sciences and Philosophy, 1920–1958.* Glencoe, Ill.: Free Press, 1959. Annotated bibliography of about 2,000 books and articles, with a 20-page section on Political Science, Public Administration and Government.

LaNoue, George R., ed. *A Bibliography of Doctoral Dissertations Undertaken in American and Canadian Universities (1940–1962) on Poli-*

tics and Religion. New York: National Council of the Churches of Christ in the U.S.A., 1963. An unannotated list of 149 dissertations in various disciplines, with "special attention to dissertations contributing information to current public policy problems in church-state relations."

Duijker, H. C. J. and N. H. Frijie. *National Character and National Stereotypes.* Amsterdam: North Holland Publishing Co., 1960. A trend report prepared for the International Union of Scientific Psychology. Has a "bibliography on national character" citing over 900 studies.

Raven, Bertram H. *A Bibliography of Publications Relating to the Small Group.* Los Angeles: Student Bookstore, Univ. of California at Los Angeles, 1965. Unannotated listing of over 3,000 articles and books.

Davis, E. E. *Attitude Change; a review and bibliography of selected research.* Paris: Unesco Reports and Papers in the Social Sciences, No. 19, 1964. "Designed to provide a review and selected bibliography of some of the more important research relevant to attempts at changing social attitudes."

Kirsch, John P. and Ronald C. Dillehay. *Dimensions of Authoritarianism; a critical review.* Lexington: Univ. of Kentucky Press, 1967. A listing and critical analysis of research and writing on authoritarianism since 1956. Covers the follow-up work to *The Authoritarian Personality.* Emphasis is on social and psychological literature, but has a section on "Political Beliefs and Behavior."

Smith, Bruce L. and Chitra M. Smith. *International Communication and Political Opinion; a guide to the literature.* Princeton: Princeton Univ. Press, 1956. An extensive bibliography, with brief annotations, emphasizing works on propaganda and public opinion. Covers writings from 1946 to 1956. Smith, Lasswell, and Casey's *Propaganda, Communication and Public Opinion; a comprehensive reference guide* (Princeton, 1946) covers the same subjects for the period 1935 to 1945. This in turn is preceded by Lasswell's *Propaganda and Promotional Activities; an annotated bibliography* (Minneapolis: Univ. of Minnesota Press, 1935). These three bibliographies can be updated to some extent through the listings in "Articles on Mass Communication in U.S. and Foreign Journals," a special bibliographical section which appears in each issue of the *Journalism Quarterly.*

Allswang, John M. and Patrick Bova. *NORC Social Research, 1941–1964; an inventory of studies and publications in social research.* Chicago: National Opinion Research Center, 1964. Describes the social surveys and other studies undertaken by the NORC from its founding in 1941 through the middle of 1964. Indicates the methodology employed in each study and lists published and unpublished materials which were based on the data of each study.

OTHER REFERENCE SOURCES

Berelson, Bernard and Gary Steiner. *Human Behavior; an inventory of scientific findings.* New York: Harcourt, Brace, 1964. A major effort to synthesize and to "present, as fully and accurately as possible, what the behavioral sciences now know about the behavior of human beings: what we really know, what we nearly know, what we think we know, what we claim to know." Has sections on Institutions; Social Stratification; Opinions, Attitudes and Beliefs, etc., which state "findings of proper generality for which there is some good amount of scientific evidence." The authors do not consider political science a behavioral science, but do include findings from the "behavioral parts" of political science.

Shaw, Marvin E. and Jack M. Wright. *Scales for the Measurement of Attitudes.* New York: McGraw-Hill, 1967. A descriptive and analytical survey of over 170 attitude scales used in social research with a section on scales measuring political attitudes.

Cantril, Hadley. *Public Opinion, 1935–1946.* Princeton: Princeton Univ. Press, 1951. A massive compilation of survey data from over 12,000 polls from 23 organizations in 16 countries for the period 1935–1946. Includes only polls based on national samples.

Public Opinion Quarterly—Cantril's compilation preceded the explosive growth of survey research in the 1950's and 1960's, and since then no one has attempted another compilation. From 1940 until 1951, however, *Public Opinion Quarterly* carried a section entitled "The Quarter's Polls" which reported all available results from major U.S. polling organizations and occasionally some polls from other countries. This feature was reinstated in the Spring, 1961, issue of *POQ,* but necessarily on a highly selected basis.

Polls. Amsterdam: N.V. Internationale Uitgeversmaatschippig "Systems Keesing," 1965– . A new quarterly periodical sponsored by the World Association of Public Opinion Research. The first issue contained data from 17 organizations in 10 countries. Sixty-two survey organizations in 20 countries have promised to cooperate by providing data. Though still highly selective, *Polls* should fill part of the gap in publication of survey research results.

Gallup Opinion Index; political, social and economic trends. Princeton: Gallup International, 1965– . A monthly compilation of data on responses to Gallup Poll questions. Each issue contains data on about 15 questions. Brings together Gallup data otherwise scattered throughout many newspapers.

International Directory of Sample Survey Centres (outside the U.S.A.). Paris: Unesco Reports and Papers in the Social Sciences, No. 17, 1962. Lists over 60 sample survey organizations in various countries, indicating the type of work they do and publications issued. Already dated as a result of the growth in this area.

DATA ARCHIVES

As noted above, the growth of survey research has far outstripped the publication of results. In combination with several other factors, particularly the availability of data in machine-readable form, this has led to a recent but rapid development of social science data archives. Though their functions vary considerably, generally these archives acquire machine-readable data from organizations and individual researchers, process the data sets, and make them available to other users for secondary analysis. The prototype of the data archive in the United States is the Roper Public Opinion Research Center, established in 1946 at Williams College. Based initially on data from the Elmo Roper polling organization, the Center now has raw data from over 6,000 studies by 22 American organizations and 71 other survey organizations overseas. The Inter-University Consortium for Political Research, founded in 1962, is a partnership arrangement through which archival data are shared among the Survey Research Center of the University of Michigan and 70 university and other research organizations in the U.S. and abroad. Several other data archives have been established within the last few years, usually in conjunction with survey research centers in leading universities.

The data archive concept is new, still in an early stage of development, and designed primarily to serve the needs of advanced researchers; consequently full treatment will not be attempted here. Students who want additional details, however, might want to check the following sources:

Rokkan, Stein, ed. *Data Archives for the Social Sciences*. Paris: Mouton, 1966. Contains papers on the production and availability of survey data and the organization and services of data archives.

Bisco, Ralph L., "Social Science Data Archives: progress and prospects," *Social Science Information*, (February, 1967), pp. 39–74. Describes about 20 general and local service archives, with information on how to obtain data from them. Also has a bibliography of writings on data archives. The bimonthly periodical, *Social Science Information*, published under the auspices of the International Social Science Council, is the best single source for current information on data archives.

Chapter 14

Public Administration, State and Local Government

The literature of public administration and state and local government is very diffuse, both in terms of substance and availability. Substantively, the old critique of research in public administration as consisting chiefly of the "how-we-do-it-here" variety of writing no longer applies; specialists in the field are striving as hard as any others in political science for theoretical and empirical generality. Partly because of its interest in the many functional areas of government, however, the primary literature in public administration is specialized and scattered.

In their literature searching, students of state and local government are confronted with a proliferation of publications emanating from thousands of local governmental units and academic or governmental research organizations. Availability and bibliographic access to state government publications are discussed in Chapter 7 of this guide. While some municipal and county governments issue lists of their own publications, there is no general bibliographic control of this output. While some sources are described in this chapter, access to governmental publications below the state level is so variable that no general discussion can be attempted here, and the student must be referred to his local library.

BIBLIOGRAPHIES

Recent Publications on Governmental Problems. Chicago: Joint Reference Lib., Public Admin. Service, 1932– . A weekly, unannotated listing of books, articles, and pamphlets on governmental problems from the federal to the local level. Each issue lists, by subject, about 100 publications.

International Review of Administrative Sciences (Revue Internationale des Sciences Administratives). Brussels: Institut Internationale des Sciences Administratives, 1928– . Each quarterly issue has a "Bibliographical Section" which contains brief abstracts of recent books on administration, plus a selected list of periodical articles. Provides reasonably good coverage of scholarly work in the field.

Mars, David and H. George Frederickson. *Suggested Library in Public Administration; with 1964 supplement.* Los Angeles: Sch. of Public Admin., Univ. of Southern California, 1964. An unannotated list of over 2,300 books and journals which the compilers believe constitute a basic library in public administration.

Spitz, Alan and Edward W. Weidner. *Development Administration; an annotated bibliography.* Honolulu: East-West Center Press, 1963. Annotated listing of about 300 periodical articles relating to administration in developing areas published between 1945 and 1960.

Heady, Ferrel and Sybil Stokes. *Comparative Public Administration; a selective annotated bibliography.* 2nd ed. Ann Arbor: Inst. of Public Admin., Univ. of Michigan, 1960. Lists and annotates over 900 books and articles relating to comparative administration on a cross-national basis.

Great Britain. Ministry of Overseas Development. Department of Technical Co-operation. *Public Administration; a select bibliography.* London, 1963. Unannotated list of over 900 books, pamphlets and articles. Compiled to assist new institutes of public administration in Africa and emphasizes material on this area. Supplements were published in 1964 and 1966 and presumably will continue to appear.

British Council. *Public Administration; a select list of books and periodicals.* London: Longmans, 1964. An unannotated listing of over 1,500 books and documents on public administration in the British Commonwealth.

United Nations. Technical Assistance Program. *International Bibliography of Public Administration*. New York: United Nations, 1957. Unannotated listing of about 1,400 books in various languages on public administration.

Seckler-Hudson, Catheryn. *Bibliography on Public Administration— Annotated*. 4th ed. Washington: American Univ. Press, 1953. Brief annotations of over 1,000 books and reports. Emphasis upon national and international administration with some attention to local administration.

Greer, Sarah. *A Bibliography of Public Administration*. New York: Inst. of Public Admin., 1926. The most extensive bibliography in the field, but now so dated as to be largely of historical interest. Part I of a revised bibliography with the same title appeared in 1933, but the revision was never completed.

U.S. Civil Service Commission. Library. *A Bibliography of Public Personnel Administration Literature*. Washington: Civil Service Commission, 1949– . An exhaustive bibliography of books, articles, documents, etc., on all aspects of public personnel administration. A basic volume was published in 1949, and eight supplements have been issued covering materials up through 1958. Since that date the bibliography can be supplemented through *Personnel Literature,* a monthly list of materials received by the Library of the Civil Service Commission.

de Grazia, Alfred. *Human Relations in Public Administration*. Chicago: Public Admin. Service, 1949. Annotated listing of about 350 items from the literature of psychology, sociology and other social sciences relating to the study of public administration.

Herndon, James and Charles Press. *A Selected Bibliography of Materials in State Government and Politics*. Lexington: Bureau of Govt. Research, Univ. of Kentucky, 1963. Lists all the relevant literature since 1945, with emphasis upon empirical and analytical studies. Arranged by state, with sections on "General Background Materials," "Political Analysis," etc. For each state there is a listing of bibliographies, in book and article form, on the government and politics of that state.

Except for one or two published since 1963 and therefore not listed in Herndon and Press, such bibliographies are not covered here.

State Government; an annotated bibliography. Chicago: Council of State Governments, 1959. Designed "to provide a listing of sources of comparative information on state laws and administrative regulations, program features and characteristics in the various fields of state operations and administrative organization."

Press, Charles. *A Bibliographic Introduction to American State Government and Politics.* East Lansing: Inst. for Community Development and Services, Michigan State Univ., 1964. A brief, unannotated list of books and articles. Sections on Comparative State Studies. Parties and Elections, Interest Groups in Legislatures, etc.

Tompkins, Dorothy C. *State Government and Administration; a bibliography.* Berkeley: Bureau of Public Admin., Univ. of California, 1954. "A guide to primary sources of information which are basic to a study of state government and administration." The most extensive bibliography on the subject, though now somewhat dated. Includes books, articles and documents classified under 18 subject areas.

Graves, W. Brooke. *American State Government and Administration.* Chicago: Council of State Governments, 1949. State-by-state listing of relevant books and reports by a leading authority in the field. Items listed are unannotated and "confined primarily to fairly substantial works" on the government of each state.

State Party Structures and Procedures; a state-by-state compendium. New York: National Municipal League, 1967. A summary of laws, regulations, and procedures by which state parties operate. Covers state and county conventions and committees, plus precinct procedures.

New Mexico. Constitutional Revision Commission. *A Selective Bibliography on State Constitutional Revision.* Albuquerque, N.M.: Sch. of Law Library, 1966. Covers recent constitutional revision activity in all states. Lists publications not included in the *Index to Legal Periodicals* and the *Monthly Checklist of State Publications.*

Texas. University. Institute of Public Affairs. *Bibliography on Texas Government.* rev. ed. Austin: Inst. of Public Affairs, Univ. of Texas,

1964. This is an extensive revision of the bibliography first issued in 1956 and listed by Herndon and Press. Lists articles, books, and documents on State and State-Local, County, and Municipal Government and on Intergovernmental Relations.

Leuthold, David A. *California Politics and Problems, 1900–1963.* Berkeley: Inst. of Governmental Studies, Univ. of California, 1965. Lists over 500 scholarly books, articles, and dissertations. Has sections on parties, interest groups, elections and campaigns.

Clem, Alan L. and George M. Platt. *A Bibliography of South Dakota Government and Politics.* Vermillion: Governmental Research Bureau, Univ. of South Dakota, 1965. Unannotated listing of books, articles, and documents published since 1951. Chiefly materials on state government administration.

Graves, W. Brooke. *Intergovernmental Relations in the United States: selected bibliography on interlocal and jurisdictional relations.* Washington: U.S. Commission on Intergovernmental Relations, 1955. An extensive but unannotated bibliography of books, documents, articles, etc., with emphasis on functional relations. Updated to some extent in the author's more recent *American Intergovernmental Relations.* (New York: Scribner, 1964).

U.S. Department of Agriculture. Economic Research Service. *A Selected Bibliography on Interlocal Governmental Cooperation.* Washington: Department of Agriculture, 1964. Annotated listing of articles and documents on cooperation among local governments, with emphasis on rural areas.

Press, Charles. *Main Street Politics; poiry-making at the local level.* East Lansing: Inst. for Community Development, Michigan State Univ., 1962. A survey of the periodical literature since 1950 on decision-making on the local government level. Covers the controversial "community studies" up to 1962 at least. Excellent analytical and critical abstracts.

Press, Charles. *Metropolitan Politics.* East Lansing: Inst. for Community Development, Michigan State Univ., 1965. A selected bibliography of about 200 books and articles on metropolitan politics.

Havighurst, Robert J. and Anton J. Jansen, "Community Research; a trend report and bibliography," *Current Sociology,* Vol. XV, No. 2, 1967. An annotated bibliography of over 400 community studies. Sections on "Theoretical Studies," "Community Studies of the Social Survey Type," and "Community Studies with a Special Focus," which has a sub-section on "Politics."

Metropolitan Area Problems; news and digest. New York: Conference on Metropolitan Area Problems, 1957– . Each bimonthly issue has a section entitled "Recent Publications on Metropolitan Area Problems," which contains a brief, highly selective listing of books and articles.

U.S. Senate. Committee on Government Operations. *Metropolitan America; a selected bibliography.* Washington: Govt. Printing Off., 1964. Annotated listing of the most significant literature on the subject.

Government Affairs Foundation. *Metropolitan Communities; a bibliography, with special emphasis on government and politics.* Chicago: Public Admin. Service, 1956. An extensive listing, with annotations, of over 5,000 items on all aspects of metropolitan government. Two supplements have been issued covering writings up through 1967.

Booth, David A. *Council-Manager Government, 1940–1964; an annotated bibliography.* Chicago: Intl. City Managers' Assn., 1965. Annotated listing of books and articles on the city manager and the council-manager plan of government published since 1940.

Bicker, William, et al. *Comparative Urban Development; an annotated bibliography.* Washington: Comparative Admin. Group, American Society for Public Admin., 1965. An annotated bibliography of over 600 books and articles published since 1950. Designed to contribute to the improvement of empirical theory in the field. The classification scheme and index provide approaches to the literature based on various theoretical concepts and empirical variables.

Halasz, D. *Metropolis; a selected bibliography on administration and other problems of metropolitan areas throughout the world.* new ed. The Hague: Nijhoff, 1967. A listing of literature on metropolitan areas outside the U.S. and Canada. Published under the auspices of the International Union of Local Authorities.

Wallace, Rosemary. *International Bibliography and Reference Guide on Urban Affairs*. Ramsey, N.J.: Ramsey-Wallace Corporation, 1966. Partially annotated subject listing of approximately 500 references on urban affairs.

OTHER REFERENCE SOURCES

See Chapter 8 for leads to statistical sources on federal, state and local governments.

Book of the States. Chicago: Council of State Governments, 1935– . Published biennially and "designed to provide an authoritative source of information on the structures, working methods, financing and functional activities of the state governments." Has sections on "Constitutions and Elections," "Legislation," "Judiciary," "Administrative Organization," "Finance," "Intergovernmental Relations," and "Major State Services." Contains a mass of descriptive and statistical data. Two supplements are issued, one a directory of "State Elective Officials and Legislatures," the other a directory of "Administrative Officials Classified by Functions."

Clements, John. *Taylor's Encyclopedia of Government Officials: federal and state*. Dallas: Taylor Publishing Co., 1967– . A directory of state and federal governmental officials and political figures. Much of the information, particularly on the federal level, can be found in other sources discussed in Chapter 12. Probably most useful for its state coverage. Lists state senators and representatives, with maps showing legislative districts. A unique feature is the lists, with addresses, of delegates to the 1964 Democratic and Republican national conventions; also lists state party chairmen. Quarterly supplements record changes and keep information up-to-date.

Index Digest of State Constitutions. 2nd ed. New York: Legislative Drafting Research Fund of Columbia Univ., 1959. Designed to present a comparative analysis and statement by subject of all provisions of the fifty state constitutions. Cumulative supplements are issued periodically which keep the *Index Digest* up to date.

Constitutions of the United States: national and state. New York: Oceana Publications for the Legislative Drafting Research Fund of Columbia Univ., 1962. A compilation of all fifty state constitutions, serving as a companion volume to the *Index Digest of State Constitutions*.

Darrah, Earl L. and Orville E. Poland. *The Fifty State Governments; a compilation of executive organization charts.* Berkeley: Bureau of Public Admin., Univ. of California, 1961. Photographic reproductions of executive organization charts of each state. An appendix contains a tabular "Comparative Analysis of State Government Organizations."

Legislative Reapportionment in the States. Chicago: Council of State Governments, 1964. Reviews significant reapportionment actions, by state, from June, 1960, to June, 1964.

Compendium on Legislative Reapportionment. 2nd ed. New York: National Municipal League, 1962. Summarizes reapportionment activity in each state as of July 1, 1961. May be updated through the National Municipal League's monthly periodical, *National Civic Review.*

Apportionment in the Nineteen Sixties: state legislatures, congressional districts. New York: National Municipal League, 1967. A compilation of historical and statistical data on the reapportionment of state legislatures and on Congressional redistricting. For each state, there is a survey of reapportionment activity since 1962, plus maps and statistical tables showing population of each legislative district and the percentage deviation from the average population. Similar information is presented for each Congressional district, based upon districts of the 90th Congress. The volume is published in loose-leaf form to facilitate updating. This source largely supersedes the two listed immediately above.

Court Decisions on Legislative Apportionment. New York: National Municipal League, 1962– . Contains the texts of all lower and Supreme Court decisions on state, Congressional and local legislative apportionment cases since the landmark *Baker v. Carr* decision of 1962. As of mid-1968, 31 volumes had been published containing over 300 decisions.

The Governors of the States, 1900–1958. Chicago: Council of State Governments, 1957. Lists governors by state, giving party and terms served. May be updated through the *Book of the States.*

Municipal Yearbook. Chicago: International City Managers' Assn., 1934– . Purpose is to provide "information on current activities and practices of cities throughout the United States." Contains extensive descriptive and statistical data on Governmental Units, Personnel, Finance, and Municipal Activities. Includes directories of mayors and other city officials. Has bibliographical sections which refer to additional sources.

Metropolitan Area Annual. Albany. Grad. Sch. of Public Affairs, State Univ. of New York at Albany, 1966– . An annual reference volume with sections on various aspects of metropolitan affairs. Has a "Metropolitan Area Bibliography," which lists recent books, articles, and pamphlets, plus a "Metropolitan Surveys" section listing studies in progress or recently completed on metropolitan problems.

Urban Affairs Annual Reviews. Beverly Hills, Calif.: Sage Pubns., Inc., 1967– . A series of "annual reference volumes designed to present critical analyses" in various fields of urban studies. Volume I is entitled *Urban Research and Policy Planning.*

Urban Research News. Beverly Hills, Calif.: Sage Pubns., Inc., 1967– . A biweekly newsletter for the urban specialist which "reports on current developments—personnel, meetings, research projects, publications, etc.—at the over 200 centers engaged in urban research."

U.S. Congress. Joint Economic Committee. *A Directory of Urban Research Study Centers.* Washington: Govt. Printing Off., 1967. A descriptive list of about 100 university and non-profit centers engaged in research on urban affairs.

American Society for Public Administration. *Society Directory.* Chicago: ASPA, 1961. An alphabetical and geographical listing of individual and institutional members of the Society.

Chapter 15

International Relations, American Foreign and Military Policy

In his recent study of the bibliographic underpinning for the field of international relations, Eric Boehm concluded: "The bibilographic situation is chaotic. We found an astounding multiplicity of different bibliographic sources. It appears that there is not a single field of knowledge in which it is so difficult to find out about published material as in the field of international relations." (*Bibliographies on International Relations and World Affairs*. Santa Barbara, Calif.: Clio Press, 1965, p. 3.)

This judgment is excessive. It is a relative matter, as in the old vaudeville bomb: "How's your wife?" "Compared to what?" If the bibliographic situation in international relations is chaotic, then many other sub-fields of political science are in sad shape indeed. The situation is difficult, but not all that impossible. The contradiction in Boehm's statement points to the problem. There are many different bibliographic sources in the field of international relations; the problem is not so much lack of coverage as picking and choosing among the sources. The advanced specialist may have his troubles in this field, particularly in gaining access to material classified for security reasons, but the literature needs of most students can be met with a little digging.

Federal government publications (see Chapter 5) are, of course, of prime importance in the study of American foreign and military policy, and any student working in these areas should become familiar with the publication output of the State and Defense Departments. Many of the sources listed in Chapter 16 on "Comparative Politics and Area Studies" will be relevant to the study of the foreign affairs of the countries or regions covered.

GUIDES TO RESEARCH

Zawodny, J. K. *Guide to the Study of International Relations*. San Francisco: Chandler Publishing Co., 1966. A well-selected list and description of the most important bibliographies, periodicals, and reference sources for the study of international relations. Arranged by type of material (encyclopedias, documents, statistical data, etc.) with subject and title indexes. The best starting point for a student new to the field and should be useful even for the specialist.

Robinson, Jacob. *International Law and Organization; general sources of information*. Leyden: A. W. Sijthoff, 1967. An excellent annotated bibliography of over 2,000 information sources—encyclopedias, dictionaries, treatises, bibliographies, yearbooks, periodicals, etc.—on public international law and organization. Supplements Zawodny, from a legal rather than political science viewpoint.

Conover, Helen F. *A Guide to Bibliographic Tools for Research in Foreign Affairs*. Washington: Lib. of Congress, 1956. A listing, with annotations, of the major bibliographies, manuals, indexes, etc., in the field. Superseded to some extent by Zawodny, but not limited to U.S. sources; has sections on Asia, Latin America, etc., which will be of some help in studying the foreign policy of other countries.

Plischke, Elmer. *American Foreign Relations; a bibliography of official sources*. College Park: Bureau of Governmental Research, Univ. of Maryland, 1955. Claims to be "the first comprehensive guide to official sources in American foreign relations." Has sections on the publications of Congress, the State Department, and other agencies which relate to American foreign policy. Lists about 800 sources and provides more detailed coverage of official U.S. sources than either Zawodny or Conover.

Bemis, Samuel F. and Grace C. Griffin. *Guide to the Diplomatic History of the United States, 1775–1921*. Washington: Govt. Printing Off., 1935. A massive guide to the printed and manuscript sources for the study of American diplomatic history. Many of the unpublished sources listed by Bemis have since been published or made available on microfilm by the National Archives. Indispensable for anyone studying American foreign relations prior to 1921 and valuable even beyond that date, since many of the sources discussed still are issued in one form or another. Part I, "Bibliography," is a descriptive listing of about 6,000 printed sources, arranged chronologically and topically. Part II, "Remarks on the Sources," provides a critical evaluation of location guides to official government sources, both printed and manuscript.

Thomas, Daniel H. and Lynn M. Case, eds. *Guide to the Diplomatic Archives of Western Europe*. Philadelphia: Univ. of Pennsylvania Press, 1959. Has a section on the archives of each country, written by a specialist. Contains details on contents, organization and accessibility of the archives, plus references to published collections of documents.

U.S. Department of State. Bureau of Intelligence and Research. Off. of External Research. *Foreign Affairs Research; a directory of governmental resources*. Washington: Govt. Printing Off., 1967. A booklet which "makes available in one publication a broad, descriptive listing of the many governmental resources accessible to the scholar who is engaged in social and behavioral science research on foreign areas and international affairs." Describes material available in or published by various agencies, with names of officials to write to for further information or permission to use the resources. This booklet supersedes a 1965 publication, *Government Resources Available for Foreign Affairs Research*.

BIBLIOGRAPHIES

Foreign Affairs Bibliography; a selected and annotated list of books on international affairs. New York: Russell & Russell, 1919–1932; R. R. Bowker, 1932–1942; 1942–1952; 1952–1962. Now in four volumes covering the years 1919–1962. Lists books only, with brief annotations, but is the most extensive general bibliography in this field. Part I is on "General International Relations" and has eight sections, including "Political Factors" and "War and Peace." Part II is on "The

World Since 1914" and Part III is entitled "The World by Regions." The bibliography can be kept up-to-date by the "Recent Books" section of the periodical *Foreign Affairs,* published quarterly by the Council on Foreign Relations.

U.S. Department of State. Bureau of Intelligence and Research. Off. of External Research. *External Research: International Affairs; a list of current social science research by private scholars and academic centers.* Washington: Department of State, 1958– . Based on the catalog of social science research on foreign areas and international affairs maintained by the Office of External Research. Contains a list of studies with brief annotations and has sections on "Government and Politics," "International Organization," "Military Affairs," etc. Until 1965 was issued in two parts, one covering "Studies in Progress," the other "Completed Studies." Since 1965, is issued annually and includes only work in progress or recently completed which is unpublished. Studies completed and published are no longer listed, but records of these are maintained by the Office of External Research in its catalog.

The Office of External Research also publishes a list of "in-house" research studies on foreign areas carried out by government agencies, but this list is classified and not widely distributed.

International Studies Quarterly. Detroit: Wayne State Univ. Press for the Intl. Studies Assn., 1957– . (Formerly entitled *Background; journal of the International Studies Association.*) In 1962, this quarterly periodical began publishing an annual bibliography of articles and books in the field of international relations. The listing was arranged by concepts and broad subjects rather than geographically, and the section on "Conceptual Schemes, Theory, and Ideas" provided some coverage of theoretical developments in the field. The bibliography did not appear in 1965 or 1966 and apparently has been discontinued.

International Organization. Boston: World Peace Foundation, 1947– . In addition to substantive articles, each quarterly issue has a "Selected Bibliography" section which lists books and articles on international organization. The listing is by a classified arrangement, with sections on "General Writings," the "United Nations," "Specialized Agencies," and "Regional Matters."

Speeckaert, G. P. *Select Bibliography on International Organization, 1885–1964.* Brussels: Union of Intl. Assns., 1965. An unannotated listing of works in various languages on "international organization in general" (350 titles) and on specific organizations (730 titles). Other bibliographies provide better coverage of major organizations such as the UN, but this source lists writings (books only, no articles) on many lesser-known, non-governmental organizations.

Douma, J. *Bibliography on the International Court of Justice Including the Permanent Court, 1918–1964.* Leyden: A. W. Sijthoff, 1965. Unannotated, but comprehensive bibliography of over 3,500 books, documents, and articles on the work, jurisdiction, and cases of the League of Nations Permanent Court of International Justice and the present UN International Court of Justice.

Moody, Margaret, ed. *Catalog of International Law and Relations.* 20 vs. Dobbs Ferry, N.Y.: Oceana Pubns., 1965–67. Reproduces the card catalog of the Harvard Law School Library's collection of materials on international law and relations. A massive bibliographical source for this field, containing over 360,000 cards allowing author, title and subject approaches to the literature.

North Atlantic Treaty Organization. *NATO Bibliography.* Paris: NATO, 1967. An unannotated, but comprehensive list of books and articles published on NATO up to February, 1967. Two chapters list works on the historical background of the NATO Treaty, while six other chapters cover the political, military, economic, legal and cultural aspects of the alliance.

U.S. Senate. Committee on Government Operations. *Organizing for National Security; studies and background materials.* Washington: Govt. Printing Off., 1961. Issued by the Subcommittee on National Policy Machinery, chaired by Senator Henry M. Jackson. Contains an extensive, annotated bibliography of books, articles and government documents on all aspects of the national security policy-making process. Supplemented by *Administration of National Security; a bibliography,* issued by the same committee in 1963.

Selected Rand Abstracts. Santa Monica, Calif.: The Rand Corporation, 1963– . Contains abstracts, with a subject index, of all unclassified Rand reports. Has sections on "Economics," "Foreign Affairs," and "Defense Policy and Strategy." Issued quarterly, with each issue cumulated into an annual volume. Indicates libraries where Rand materials are deposited and how to order individual reports. The *Index of Se-lected Publications of the Rand Corporation,* published in 1962, lists unclassified Rand reports from 1946 through 1962.

Air University Abstracts of Student Research Reports. Maxwell Air Force Base, Ala.: Air Univ. Library, 1957– . Contains abstracts, with a subject index, of reports done by student officers at the Air War College and other Air Force schools.

Social Science Research Council. Committee on Civil Military Relations. *Civil-Military Relations; an annotated bibliography, 1940–1952.* New York: Columbia Univ. Press, 1954. A bibliography of books, articles, documents and other writings in English published between 1940 and the end of 1952.

Lang, Kurt. "Military Sociology; a trend report and bibliography," *Current Sociology,* Vol. XIII, No. 1, 1965. A critical essay on recent writing on military sociology, plus a bibliography of over 500 articles and books.

Crawford, Elizabeth T. *The Social Sciences in International and Military Policy; an analytic bibliography.* Washington: Bureau of Social Science Research, 1965. An annotated bibliography of 150 books, articles and reports pertaining to the role of social science research in international relations and military policy since the beginning of World War II.

U.S. Department of the Army. Army Library. *U.S. Security, Arms Control, and Disarmament, 1961–1965.* Washington: Govt. Printing Off., 1966. Lists, with extensive annotations, over 700 books, articles, documents, and unclassified reports on these subjects published between 1961 and 1965. An earlier publication with the same title covers the years 1960 and 1961.

U.S. Department of State. Bureau of Intelligence and Research. Off. of External Research. *Arms Control and Disarmament; studies in progress or recently completed.* Washington: Department of State, 1963– . A semi-annual listing of research in progress or recently completed on all aspects of the subject. The best single bibliographic source for published writings on disarmament and arms control is the quarterly abstract, *Arms Control and Disarmament,* described in Chapter 3.

U.S. Department of the Army. Army Library. *Disarmament; a bibliographic record, 1916–1960.* Washington: Govt. Printing Off., 1961. Lists and annotates books, documents and articles "reflective of the policies, trends and methods of negotiations on both sides of the disarmament table."

United Nations. Secretariat. *Disarmament: a select bibliography, 1962–1964.* New York: United Nations, 1965. An extensive listing of writings on the technical, social, political and other aspects of disarmament published from 1962 through 1964.

Clemens, Walter C., Jr. *Soviet Disarmament Policy, 1917–1963; an annotated bibliography of Soviet and Western sources.* Stanford, Calif.: Hoover Inst., 1965. An annotated listing of the most important primary and secondary materials on Soviet disarmament policy which have appeared in Russia, Europe, and America from 1917 to 1963. Includes 820 items, arranged chronologically and topically, with separate sections for Communist and Western writings.

U.S. Department of the Army. *Nuclear Weapons and the Atlantic Alliance; a bibliographic survey.* Washington: Govt. Printing Off., 1965. Abstracts over 700 books, articles and documents on NATO and nuclear weapons. A short bibliography on Chinese nuclear power appears as an appendix.

U.S. Department of the Army. *Civil Defense, 1960–1967; a bibliographic survey.* Washington: Govt. Printing Off., 1967. An annotated bibliography of several hundred books, articles and official documents on the military, technical, political and social aspects of civil defense. Appendices contain some statistical data on civil defense.

U.S. Department of the Army. *Strength in Reserve; a bibliographic survey of the United States Army Reserve.* Washington: Govt. Printing Off., 1968. An annotated bibliography of 500 writings, intended as a "comprehensive compilation of materials on the historical, organizational, operational, and legislative aspects of the Army Reserve."

U.S. Department of the Army. *Civilians in Peace, Soldiers in War; a bibliographic survey of the Army and Air National Guard.* Washington: Govt. Printing Off., 1967. An annotated bibliography of about 900 articles, documents, etc., on the military and political aspects of the Guard. Appendices contain directories and statistical data.

U.S. Department of the Army. Office of the Adjutant General. *Military Manpower Policy; a bibliographic survey*. Washington: Govt. Printing Off., 1965. Annotated list of over 700 writings on all aspects of U.S. military manpower policy, including the draft, reserves, service personnel policies, etc. Classified into 9 broad subject sections, with author and subject indexes.

Halperin, Morton H. *Limited War; an essay on the development of the theory and an annotated bibliography*. Cambridge: Center for Intl. Studies, Harvard Univ., 1962. Covers over 300 books and articles, constituting all public writings on limited war which had come to the author's attention up to January, 1962.

Condit, D. M., et al. *A Counterinsurgency Bibliography*. Washington: Special Operations Research Off., American Univ., 1963. A 300-page annotated bibliography on "fundamental elements" and "historical models" of counterinsurgency, prepared on contract for the Army. Covers English-language unclassified literature up to mid-1962. Seven supplements, the last published in June, 1965, appeared under the title *Counterinsurgency Bibliography*. Beginning with Supplement No. 8 in February, 1966, this series was merged with two other bibliographic supplements (see below) under the title *Bibliography on Counterinsurgency, Unconventional Warfare, and Psychological Operations;* updated supplements are published about every six months. In 1966, following the flap over "Project Camelot" and other Army-sponsored research in Latin America, the Special Operations Research Office (SORO) changed its name to the Center for Research in Social Systems (CRESS).

Berger, Carl and Howard C. Reese. *Psychological Operations; bibliography*. Washington: Special Operations Research Off., American Univ., 1960. An annotated bibliography of writings on psychological warfare and related subjects published over the last fifty years. Seven supplements were published, the last in August, 1965, under the title *A Psychological Operations Bibliography,* then were merged with the general supplement mentioned above (see Condit).

Miller, Hope, et al. *A Selected Bibliography on Unconventional Warfare*. Washington: Special Operations Research Off., American Univ., 1961. A 137-page annotated bibliography which "presents a cross-section of available literature on the interrelated fields of guerilla warfare, evasion-and-escape, and subversion." Seven supplements were issued under the title *Unconventional Warfare Bibliography,* then the series was merged under the general supplement listed above (see Condit).

Annotated Bibliography of CRESS Publications. Washington: Center for Research in Social Systems, American Univ., 1966. A list and index of technical reports, bibliographies, and other publications issued by CRESS and its predecessor agency, SORO.

U.S. Air Force Academy. Library. *Unconventional Warfare Series.* Boulder, Colo. Air Force Academy Lib. An unannotated bibliography of books and articles. Appears as part of the Library's "Special Bibliography Series" and consists of four separate numbers on *Guerilla Warfare, Psychological Warfare, Escape and Evasion,* and *Propaganda.*

Riddleburger, Peter B. *Military Roles in Developing Countries; an inventory of past research and analysis.* Washington: Special Operations Research Off., American Univ., 1965. A 182-page annotated bibliography, arranged by geographic region, of writings on the function of the military in developing areas.

U.S. Department of State. Bureau of Intelligence and Research. Off. of External Research. *Role of the Military in the Less Developed Countries, January 1959 to February 1964; a selected bibliography.* Washington: Department of State, 1964. A brief list of studies completed or in progress on the role of the armed forces and military elites in Africa, Asia, Latin America, and the Middle East.

U.S. Department of State. Bureau of Intelligence and Research. Off. of External Research. *Soviet Military Doctrine; a list of references to recent Soviet and Free World publications on Soviet military thought.* Washington: Department of State, 1963. "A selected list of recent Soviet and Free World publications on Soviet military thought on strategic and tactical principles for a future general war." Includes about 400 sources, divided into sections on "Communist Writings" and "Free World Writings."

U.S. Pacific Air Forces. *PACAF Bibliographies for Base Librarians: Intelligence.* San Francisco: Commander-in-Chief, Pacific Air Forces, 1965. An annotated list of recent popular and some academic writing on intelligence organizations and activities. A supplement to the bibliography was issued in October, 1966.

Gray, Charles, et al. *A Bibliography of Peace Research Indexed by Key Words*. Eugene, Ore.: General Research Analysis Methods, 1968. A "Key Word in Context" index to all articles on peace research appearing in *Journal of Conflict Resolution, Journal of Peace Research* and other journals in this field.

Legault, Albert. *Peace-Keeping Operations; a bibliography*. Paris: Intl. Information Center on Peace-Keeping Operations, 1967. A bibliography, with extensive English-language annotations, of several hundred books, articles and official documents on peace-keeping operations. Emphasis is on the United Nations' activities in this field.

Williams, Stillman P. *Toward a Genuine World Security System; an annotated bibliography for layman and scholar*. Washington: United World Federalists, 1964. Annotated bibliography of 355 books and articles, mainly published in the 1960's, on "world law, world order, and world peace." Classified under 16 subject areas, with an author index.

Miller, William R. *Bibliography of Books on War, Pacifism, Non-violence and Related Studies*. Nyack, N.Y.: Fellowship of Reconciliation, 1961. A list, with brief annotations, of about 500 books and pamphlets, generally reflecting a pacifist viewpoint, thought "to be useful to serious students of the nature and causes of war and of alternatives to it."

Carter, April, et al. *Non-violent Action; theory and practice; a selected bibliography*. London: Housmans, 1966. Lists 277 writings in English on non-violent resistance movements and theorists of non-violent action.

OTHER REFERENCE SOURCES

Deadline Data on World Affairs. New York: Deadline Data, Inc. A current awareness service reporting on the foreign and domestic affairs of "every country in the world, every crisis and every significant world issue." Distributed in card format rather than the usual magazine format and updated by weekly revisions. In 1963, Deadline Data, Inc. began publishing a monthly periodical, *On Record*, with each issue focusing on a particular country or event and containing background data and a chronological summary. Since 1966, however, this service is also available only in card format.

International Review Service. New York: Intl. Review Service, Inc., 1954– . A periodical published five or six times a year, with each issue covering a specific topic—Chinese representation in the UN, the Rhodesian crisis, etc.—with background information and chronological summary of events. A summary of United Nations activities appears once a year.

Year Book of World Affairs. London: Stevens & Sons for the London Inst. of World Affairs, 1947– . Not a "current awareness" service like those listed above. Each annual volume contains long descriptive and analytical articles on major world developments, written by academic specialists.

Survey of International Affairs. London: Oxford Univ. Press for the Royal Inst. of Intl. Affairs, 1920– . An authoritative series of annual volumes reviewing events of international importance throughout the world. Coverage varies, but each volume usually leads off with general analytical articles followed by sections on regions or countries. A companion series, *Documents on International Affairs* (1928–) contains the full text of major documents, foreign policy statements, and communiques of the various governments. There is a time lag of about five years in the publication of both series; the 1961 volume of the *Survey* appeared in 1965 .

The United States in World Affairs. New York: Harper & Row for the Council on Foreign Relations, 1931– . A series of annual volumes, the purpose being "to present a concise analytical record of the American international experience" during the year. A companion series, *Documents on American Foreign Relations* (1939–) "makes available in convenient reference form the most important documentary materials concerning the foreign relations of the United States" during the year.

U.S. Department of State. *Foreign Relations of the United States: diplomatic papers.* Washington: Govt. Printing Off., 1861– . The primary source for study of U.S. foreign relations. The series, now running to over 180 volumes, contains diplomatic communications between Washington and U.S. embassies overseas, diplomatic notes and memoranda, reports, and much other material. There is a general index covering the volumes up through 1918, with separate indexes in each volume since that date. Arrangement of the contents varies but is generally by geographic area. Officially, the time lag for release and publication of diplomatic papers in this series is 15 years, but it now stretches beyond 20 years; the volumes covering 1945 are just now being published. For a discussion of the series, see Richard W. Leopold's article, "The Foreign Relations Series; a centennial estimate," appearing in the *Mississippi Valley Historical Review* for March, 1963.

Even the *Foreign Relations* series, massive as it is, necessarily is only a selection of relevant documents. Many documents in the State Department archives were not included at the time of publication because of lack of space, a judgment that they were not important enough, or—on occasion—out of diplomatic caution. In recent years, however, practically the full archive up through 1929 has been made available on microfilm. Because of the cost, no single library is likely to have all this material; the file on U.S. relations with Russia from 1910 to 1929, for example, runs to over 200 reels of microfilm. For a list of all materials available, however, see the *List of National Archives Microfilm Publications, 1968,* issued by the U.S. National Archives and Records Service.

Several official publications bring the *Foreign Relations* series up to date, at least to the extent of including the most important and most public foreign policy materials. The weekly *State Department Bulletin* contains very recent policy statements, treaties, communiques, etc. This is supplemented by an annual State Department publication, *American Foreign Policy: Current Documents,* issued since 1956. For the years prior to 1956 there is *A Decade of American Foreign Policy: Basic Documents, 1941–1949,* published by the Senate Foreign Relations Committee, plus a State Department supplement covering the years 1950–1955.

U.S. Department of State. *United States Treaties and Other International Agreements.* Washington: Govt. Printing Off., 1950–   . Contains the texts of all treaties, conventions, executive agreements, etc., to which the United States is a party. Prior to 1950, the same materials appeared in the *U.S. Statutes at Large.* For more detail on the publication and location of treaties, see Chapter 13, "Foreign Affairs," of Laurence F. Schmeckebier and Roy B. Eastin, *Government Publications and Their Use.* rev. ed. Washington: Brookings Institution, 1961.

U.S. Department of State. *Treaties in Force; a list of treaties and other international agreements of the United States in force*. Washington: Govt. Printing Off., 1929– . Published annually. Part I lists bilateral treaties and other agreements by country. Part II lists multilateral treaties and agreements by subject. Both parts cite original sources where texts of the treaties and agreements may be found.

Great Britain. Foreign Office. *British and Foreign State Papers*. London: H.M. Stationery Off., 1813– . A series of annual volumes containing the most important documents which have been made public on British foreign policy and relations with other countries. Each volume has a subject index and chronological list of documents, and there are several cumulative indexes covering various time periods. There is a time lag of several years; the volume for 1959–60 was published in 1967. These volumes are roughly the British equivalent of the U.S. State Department series *American Foreign Policy: Current Documents* and contain only materials which the government wishes to make public. The British are even more restrictive than the U.S. government in releasing and publishing confidential diplomatic papers. For a discussion of British practice and sources, see D. C. Watt, "Foreign Affairs, the Public Interest and the Right to Know," *Political Quarterly,* April, 1963.

Great Britain. Foreign Office. *Documents on British Foreign Policy, 1919–1939*. London: H.M. Stationery Off. Contains texts of "the most important documents in the Foreign Office Archives relating to British foreign policy between 1919 and 1939." Divided into three series totalling 32 volumes, with each series covering different time spans; Volume X of the third series is a general index. Publication was a departure from usual British practice and resulted from a decision to make available materials on British policy during the inter-war period.

U.S. Department of State. *Documents on German Foreign Policy, 1918– 1945; from the archives of the German Foreign Ministry*. Washington: Govt. Printing Off. The Germans were unfortunate enough to lose the last war and to have the records of their Foreign Ministry captured by American troops. This collection contains English translations of the most important papers and documents of the German Foreign Ministry and Reich Chancellery. Planned to cover the entire 1918–1945 period, the collection to date covers only 1933–1941, in two series of 19 volumes. It is highly selective, containing only a very small proportion of all documents captured. Much of the other material, however, has been microfilmed and is available in German from the Library of Congress or other sources. For a catalog, subject index, and finding list of the microfilmed materials, see George O. Kent, ed., *A Catalog of Files and Microfilms of the German Foreign Ministry Archives, 1920–1945.* 3 vs. Stanford, Calif.: Hoover Inst., 1962–1966.

Degras, Jane T., ed. *Soviet Documents on Foreign Policy.* London: Oxford Univ. Press, 1951–1953. Three volumes covering the period 1917–1941. Contains English translations of major government and party statements, diplomatic notes, speeches, and Tass statements.

Eudin, Xenia and Robert M. Slusser. *Soviet Foreign Policy, 1928–1934; documents and materials.* Vol. I. University Park, Pa.: Pennsylvania State Univ. Press for the Hoover Inst., 1966. Contains a narrative summary and 70 documents presenting "the most important points of the Soviet communists' own evaluation of their foreign policies and their general interpretation of the world situation in the period 1928–1934." A continuation of Eudin and H. H. Fisher, *Soviet Russia and the West, 1920–1927; a documentary survey* and Eudin and R. C. North, *Soviet Russia and the East, 1920–1927; a documentary survey,* both published in 1957 by the Stanford University Press.

Jados, Stanley S. *Documents on Russian-American Relations; Washingington to Eisenhower.* Washington: Catholic Univ. of America Press, 1965. A collection of the most important documents reflecting relations between the U.S. and Russia, arranged chronologically by President.

Yearbook of International Organizations. Brussels: Union of Intl. Assns., 1948–   . Gives members, officers, history, structure, etc., of both intergovernmental and non-governmental organizations. Since 1962–63 the Union has issued a separate *Who's Who in International Organizations,* which is an index to all individuals listed in the *Yearbook.* The Union's monthly periodical, *International Associations,* carries current news of the activities of international organizations.

Peaslee, Amos J. *International Governmental Organizations: constitutional documents.* 2nd ed. The Hague: Martinus Nijhoff, 1961. Contains texts of charters and other founding documents of multilateral governmental organizations, with brief summary of purpose and activities.

Peaslee, Amos J. *Constitutions of Nations*. 2nd ed. The Hague: Martinus Nijhoff, 1956. "The first compilation in English of the texts of the constitutions of the various nations of the world, together with summaries, annotations, bibliography, and comparative tables." A third edition is scheduled to be published shortly.

U.S. Department of State. *The Biographic Register*. Washington: Govt. Printing Off., 1870– . An annual directory providing brief biographical information on State Department personnel, Foreign Service officers, and officials of other agencies such as USIA, the Peace Corps, and AID, who participate in American foreign operations. A brief bureaucratic controversy arose over this publication during the summer of 1966. The CIA objected to it because the biographical information might make it possible to spot CIA men operating under the cover of American embassies abroad. One day a subordinate official of the State Department announced that the *Biographic Register* would no longer be published, only to be reversed the next day by higher authority. It was said that State considered the identity of "spooks" operating under its cover to be something less than a secret to the Russians, Chinese and natives of the countries concerned. The *Foreign Service List* (1857–), issued twice a year by the State Department, lists by country the personnel assigned to foreign posts. The student who wants a little diversion might take the *Foreign Service List,* compare it with the *Biographic Register,* and see how many ghosts he can spot. The State Department's *Diplomatic List* (1894–) gives names and addresses of diplomatic officials from other countries accredited to the U.S. government.

Haensch, Gunther. *Dictionary of International Relations and Politics*. New York: Elsevier Publishing Co., 1965. Gives definitions and word equivalents in English, French, German and Spanish of over 5,000 terms encountered in the international relations field.

Council on Foreign Relations. *American Agencies Interested in International Affairs*. New York: Praeger, 1964. Lists "those private organizations which conduct serious programs of research in international affairs, or which maintain meetings and information programs on a continuing basis." Gives officers, addresses, statement of purpose, activities, etc.

U.S. Department of State. Office of External Research. *University Centers of Foreign Affairs Research; a directory*. Washington: Govt. Printing Off., 1968. A directory of 191 "university-affiliated centers which have as their main purpose social science research in foreign affairs." For each center, address, director, description of program, and list of recent publications or studies in progress are given.

The Military Balance. London: Inst. of Strategic Studies, 1958– . An "annual estimate of the nature and size of the military forces of the principal powers." Has sections on "The Communist Powers," "The Western Alliances" and "The Non-Aligned Countries." Also contains comparative tables on defense expenditures, major nuclear delivery systems, and other components of military power.

Reference Handbook of the Armed Forces of the World. Washington: Robert C. Sellers & Associates, 1966– . Contains data on the defense budgets, manpower, and equipment of the armed forces of each country. A new publication similar to, though perhaps less authoritative than, *The Military Balance*.

Brassey's Annual. London: William Clowes & Sons, Ltd., 1886– . Each volume has several articles on military and strategic matters, chiefly by British and American specialists. Has a bibliography of recent books and articles, plus statistical and other data on the British armed forces.

Schwarz, Urs and Laszlo Hadik. *Strategic Terminology; a trilingual glossary*. New York: Praeger, 1966. Defines about 300 key strategic military-political terms currently in use, giving equivalents in English, French and German. Cites examples of use by writers in the field, keyed to a brief bibliographical appendix. For the political scientist, probably the most useful of the dictionaries listed here.

U.S. Joint Chiefs of Staff. *A Dictionary of United States Military Terms*. Washington: Foreign Affairs Press, 1963. Defines about 3,000 terms, symbols and acronyms for use by the U.S. military and NATO. A mixture of strategic terminology and "nuts and bolts" military usage.

Noel, Captain Jack V. *Naval Terms Dictionary*. 2nd ed. Annapolis, Md.: United States Naval Inst., 1966. One-line definitions of current naval terminology, chiefly of the "nuts and bolts" variety. Has separate sections listing aircraft and ship designations.

International Repertory of Institutions Specializing in Research on Peace and Disarmament. Paris: Unesco Reports and Papers in the Social Sciences, No. 23, 1966. Lists and describes the work of over 80 national and international research organizations in this field, including lists of their current research projects and most important publications.

Willkie, Lloyd and Laird Willcox. *International Peace/Disarmament Directory.* 2nd ed. York, Pa.: The Authors, 711 South Duke St., 1963. A list, with addresses, of about 1,400 "organizations and individuals working for peace and disarmament." Also lists about 350 periodicals containing "peace/disarmament material."

Chapter **16**

Comparative Politics
and Area Studies

These sub-fields have a more extensive bibliographical apparatus than any others in political science, in large part because of the impetus given to area studies by the federal government and the interest of other disciplines in these areas. Though the new developments in comparative politics have not yet received adequate bibliographic attention, within the last 10 to 15 years numerous bibliographies and reference sources on specific regions and countries have appeared. Many of the sources listed below are not limited to political science materials but cover several disciplines. Only English-language sources are listed, but many of these in turn cover materials in other languages which the advanced student might want to consult.

Chapter 9 of this guide, on "English-Language Translations of Foreign Sources," may be of interest, as well as Chapter 8 on "Statistical Sources." Also, readers should remember that the seven bibliographies in the "General Sources" section below which deal with the British Empire, the Commonwealth and the Colonial Office will be applicable to most if not all of the following sections, since the Empire in one way or another touched on the affairs of almost every country in the world. Where those bibliographies are specifically relevant, a note has been placed at the head of the section.

GENERAL SOURCES COVERING SEVERAL AREAS

BIBLIOGRAPHIES AND OTHER REFERENCE SOURCES

A Select Bibliography: Asia, Africa, Eastern Europe, Latin America.
New York: American Universities Field Staff, 1960. Lists about 6,000
books in Western languages on these areas. Many titles are briefly
annotated, and letters "A" and "B" in the margins indicate books
which the editors consider most important. Three supplements have
been published which bring the listing up to 1965, and apparently
future supplements will appear every two years.

Journal of Developing Areas. Macomb: Western Illinois Univ. Press,
1966– . Each issue of this quarterly journal carries a section entitled
"Bibliography of Periodicals and Monographs," which lists, by region,
recent articles and books on developing areas.

U.S. Department of State. Bureau of Intelligence and Research. *Political
Development; a bibliography, 1960–1965* rev. ed. Washington: Department of State, 1965. "This bibliography has . . . been prepared
to suggest some of the important books and articles which have been
published from January, 1960 to May, 1964 on political development
problems."

Carnell, Francis. *The Politics of the New States; a select annotated bibliography with special reference to the Commonwealth.* New York: Oxford Univ. Press, 1961. Compiled as a "rudimentary guide for those
who are interested in the politics of the developing areas as a whole."
Lists about 1,600 books and articles.

Hazlewood, Arthur. *The Economics of Development; an annotated list
of books and articles published 1958–1962.* London: Oxford Univ.
Press, 1964. Lists over 700 English-language writings, chiefly economic, but with a section on Government. Two earlier editions of this
work appeared under the title *The Economics of Under-Developed
Areas.*

Rokkan, Stein and J. Viet. *Comparative Survey Analysis; an annotated
bibliography.* Paris: Intl. Committee for Social Sciences Documentation, 1962. A mimeographed bibliography of cross-national survey
research conducted prior to 1962.

Comparative Political Studies. Beverly Hills, Calif.: Sage Pubns., 1968– . Every other issue of this quarterly journal carries a section entitled "Recent Studies in Comparative Politics—an annotated listing," which lists recent books and articles in the field.

ReQua, Eloise and Jane Statham. *The Developing Nations; a guide to information sources.* Detroit: Gale Research Co., 1965. An annotated bibliography of books, articles, and other sources. Emphasis is on economic materials, but has sections on political and social development.

Minnesota Univ. Department of Political Science. Center for Comparative Political Analysis. *Bibliography on Planned Social Change.* 3 vs. Minneapolis: Univ. of Minnesota, 1967. Volume I is an annotated bibliography of over 1,000 articles, in English, published from 1955 through 1965. The emphasis is on rural development and education in developing areas, but there is considerable material relevant to political development and comparative politics. A coded indexing system provides subject and geographical approaches. Volume II annotates about 600 books and monographs on social change, with a section on "Political Development." Volume III covers U.S. and UN publications on the subject, plus special conference proceedings.

Kabir, A. K. *Social Change and Nation Building in the Developing Areas; a selected annotated bibliography.* Dacca, Pakistan: National Inst. of Public Admin., 1965. An annotated bibliography of 66 books and articles on "Theories and Models of Development," "The Process of Development" and "Development Assistance." Highly selective.

Matthews, Daniel. *The New Afro-Asian States in Perspective, 1960–1963.* Washington: African Bibliographic Center, 1965. An unannotated listing of recent books and articles, primarily in English, on Afro-Asian countries.

The Commonwealth Office Year Book. London: Her Majesty's Stationery Off., 1967– . A general handbook on the organization and agencies of the Commonwealth, with separate sections on each country and some statistical and directory information. The Commonwealth Relations Office and the Colonial Office merged in 1966, and this yearbook supersedes the former *Colonial Office List* and *Commonwealth Relations Office Year Book.*

Flint, John E. *Books on the British Empire and Commonwealth; a guide for students.* London: Oxford Univ. Press, 1968. An unannotated bibliography of books, chiefly those published since 1940, with emphasis on historical and political works. Arranged by country.

Great Britain. Colonial Office Lib. *Catalogue of the Colonial Office Library.* Boston: G. K. Hall, 1964. Reproduces the card catalog of the Colonial Office Library, which has a large collection of materials on the countries of the former British Empire and Commonwealth. Contains over 176,000 cards providing author, subject and title approaches to the literature. A *Supplement* covering the Library's accessions for the years 1963–1967 was published in 1967.

Horne, A. J. *The Commonwealth Today; a select bibliography on the Commonwealth and its constituent countries.* London: The Library Assn., 1965. A listing, briefly annotated, of 720 recent books. Arranged by country, with a section on "Government and Politics" for each country. Coverage is similar to Flint, though with more emphasis on very recent writings.

Livingston, William S., ed. *Federalism in the Commonwealth; a bibliographical commentary.* London: Cassell for the Hansard Society, 1963. A series of bibliographical essays, citing an extensive body of literature, on federalism in various countries of the Commonwealth.

Liboiran, Albert A. *Federalism and Intergovernmental Relations in Australia, Canada, the United States and Other Countries; a bibliography.* Kingston, Ontario: Inst. of Intergovernmental Relations, Queen's Univ., 1967. "This bibliography is an attempt to bring under one cover the vast number of books, pamphlets and articles (on federalism and intergovernmental relations) that have appeared over the past one hundred years." Unannotated listing of over 3,500 sources.

Mansergh, Nicholas, ed. *Documents and Speeches on Commonwealth Affairs, 1952–1962.* London: Oxford Univ. Press, 1963. A collection of the most important speeches and official documents on Commonwealth affairs. Has sections on "Constitutional Structure and Membership," "External Policies," "Economic and Social Policies," and "The Commonwealth: Organization and Purposes." The period 1931–1952 is covered by Mansergh's *Documents and Speeches on British Commonwealth Affairs,* published in 1953.

Beginning in the early 1960's, the Foreign Areas Studies Division of the Special Operations Research Office (now the Center for Research on Social Systems) of American University issued a series of *U.S. Army Area Handbooks* for various countries. Research and compilation of the handbooks were funded by the Army, and they were published by the Government Printing Office as official government documents. Each handbook has a common organization and format, with sections entitled "Social Background," "Political Background," "Economic Background" and "Military Background." In most of the handbooks, the sections on "Political Background" have chapters entitled "Constitution and Government," "Political Dynamics," "Public Information," "Foreign Relations" and "Attitudes and Reactions of the People." In some cases there are additional chapters on "Public Order and Safety," "Subversive Potential" and "Domestic Indoctrination and External Propaganda." In all cases, each section has an attached "Selected Bibliography" of books and articles recommended for further reading.

The common introductory section of each handbook explains the background and purpose of the series:

"This volume is one of a series of handbooks prepared by the Foreign Areas Studies Division (FASD) of The American University, designed to be useful to military and other personnel who need a convenient compilation of basic facts about the social, economic, political and military institutions and practices of various countries. The emphasis is on objective description of the nation's present society and the kinds of possible or probable change that might be expected in the future. The handbook seeks to present as full and as balanced an integrated exposition as limitations on space and research time permit. It was compiled from information available in openly published material. Extensive bibliographies are provided to permit recourse to other published sources for more detailed information. There has been no attempt to express any specific point of view or to make policy recommendations. The contents of the handbook represent the work of the authors and FASD and do not represent the official view of the United States Government."

The handbooks, running from 400 to 600 pages each, are issued as Army Department Pamphlets. Those published so far are listed below, with date of publication and pamphlet number:

U.S. Army Area Handbook for Algeria. 1965. pamphlet 550–44.

... *Angola.* 1967. pamphlet 550–59.

... *Burma.* 1968. pamphlet 550–61.

... *Cambodia.* 2nd ed. 1968. pamphlet 550–50.

... *Colombia.* 1961. pamphlet 550–26.

... *Communist China.* 1967. pamphlet 550–60.

... *Cyprus.* 1964. pamphlet 550–22.

... *Dominican Republic.* 1966. pamphlet 550–54.

... *Ecuador.* 1966. pamphlet 550–52.

... *Ethiopia.* 2nd ed. 1964. pamphlet 550–28.

... *Germany.* 2nd ed. 1964. pamphlet 550–29.

... *India.* 1964. pamphlet 550–21.

... *Indonesia.* 1964. pamphlet 550–39.

... *Japan.* 2nd ed. 1964. pamphlet 550–30.

... *Kenya.* 1967. pamphlet 550–56.

... *Korea.* 1964. pamphlet 550–41.

... *Laos.* 1967. pamphlet 550–58.

... *Liberia.* 1964. pamphlet 550–38.

... *Malaysia and Singapore.* 1965. pamphlet 550–45.

... *Morocco.* 1965. pamphlet 550–49.

... *Nepal (with Sikkim and Bhutan).* 1964. pamphlet 550–35.

... *North Vietnam.* 1967. pamphlet 550–57.

... *Pakistan.* 1965. pamphlet 550–48.

... *Peru.* 1965. pamphlet 550–42.

... *Republic of the Sudan.* 2nd ed. 1964. pamphlet 550–27.

... *Saudi Arabia.* 1966. pamphlet 550–51.

... *South Vietnam.* 1967. pamphlet 550–55.

... *Syria.* 1965. pamphlet 550–47.

... *Tanzania.* 1968. pamphlet 550–62.

... *Thailand.* 2nd ed. 1968. pamphlet 550–53.

... *United Arab Republic (Egypt).* 1964. pamphlet 550–43.

SOVIET UNION AND EASTERN EUROPE

BIBLIOGRAPHIES

Horecky, Paul L. *Russia and the Soviet Union; a bibliographic guide to Western-language publications.* Chicago: Univ. of Chicago Press, 1965. "A conspectus of those Western-language writings, chiefly in book form, which are considered to be particularly relevant to the study of the political, socio-economic, and intellectual life in the Russian Empire and in the Soviet Union." Has sections on "History," "The State," "Economic and Social Structure," etc. A chapter on "General Reference Aids and Bibliographies" lists many sources not covered in this guide.

Horecky, Paul L. *Basic Russian Publications; an annotated bibliography on Russia and the Soviet Union.* Chicago: Univ. of Chicago Press, 1962. A companion volume to the work listed above, but covering Russian-language sources only.

Maichel, Karol. *Guide to Russian Reference Books.* Stanford, Calif.: The Hoover Inst., 1962– . An annotated guide to reference materials in both Russian and Western languages. Two volumes published to date, one covering "General Bibliographies and Reference Books," the other covering "History, Geography, and Ethnology." Several other volumes are scheduled to be published, one of which will cover "Social Science."

American Bibliography of Russian and East European Studies. Bloomington: Indiana Univ. Russian and East European Series, 1956– . An annual listing of "all works of professional interest pertaining to Russia and East Europe published in America or by Americans anywhere in the world." Has sections on "Political Science," "International Relations," "Law," etc. Includes periodical articles as well as books, but has no annotations. Recent volumes have attempted to include all English-language writing, not just works by Americans. Earlier coverage of writings on East Europe is provided by Robert F. Byrnes, *Bibliography of American Publications on East Central Europe, 1945–1957* (Bloomington: Indiana Univ. Publications. Slavic and East European Series, Vol. 12, 1958).

U.S. Department of State. Bureau of Intelligence and Research. Office of External Research. *External Research: USSR and East Europe.* Washington: Department of State, 1952– . Lists research currently in progress by private scholars and academic centers. Has sections on "Government and Politics," "Foreign Relations," "Press and Propaganda," and other subjects.

U.S. Department of the Army. *Soviet Russia; strategic survey: a bibliography.* Washington: Govt. Printing Off., 1963. An annotated bibliography of about 1,000 books and articles "that reflect on the strategic, political, and economic status of the Soviet Union as a world power intent on extending its influence beyond its national borders and dominating the world." Sources classified into eight subject areas, with sections on "National Policy, Strategy, and Objectives;" "The Soviet State: government and party;" "Sources of Military Power," etc. The appendices list Congressional documents on Soviet Russia and contain statistical data on the Soviet armed forces.

Armstrong, John A. *An Essay on Sources for the Study of the Communist Party of the Soviet Union, 1934–1960.* Washington: Department of State, 1962. A bibliographical essay on materials used by the author in preparing his book, *The Politics of Totalitarianism.* Refers to English- and Russian-language sources.

Harvard University Library. *Russian History Since 1917.* Cambridge: Harvard Univ. Press, 1966. (Widener Library Shelflist, No. 4.) An unannotated listing of books on history of the Soviet period in the Harvard Library. There are separate listings by author, classification number, and by date of publication.

Carson, George B. *Russia Since 1917.* Washington: American Historical Assn. Service Center for Teachers of History, 1962. A brief essay on major English-language histories of Soviet Russia.

Butler, William E. *Writings on Soviet Law and Soviet International Law; a bibliography of books and articles published since 1917 in languages other than East European.* Cambridge, Mass.: Harvard Univ. Law Sch. Lib., 1966. An unannotated listing of 3,300 articles, books, etc., on the Soviet legal system and Soviet international law.

U.S. Library of Congress. *The USSR and Eastern Europe; periodicals in Western languages.* 3rd ed. Washington: Govt. Printing Off., 1967. An annotated listing, by country, of 769 periodicals in English, German,

French and other Western languages dealing with Russia and the various countries of Eastern Europe.

Dossick, Jesse J. *Doctoral Research on Russia and the Soviet Union.* New York: New York Univ. Press, 1960. An unannotated listing of dissertations, primarily American, on all subjects. Current dissertations on Russia are listed annually in the *Slavic Review,* beginning with the December, 1964, issue.

McNeal, Robert H. *Stalin's Works; an annotated bibliography.* Stanford, Calif.: Hoover Inst., 1967. (Hoover Inst. Bibliographical Series, No. 26.) A listing of all known writings by Stalin (1,018 in all), with citations as to their location, including English translations when available.

Prpic, George J. *Eastern Europe and World Communism; a selective annotated bibliography in English.* Cleveland, Ohio: Inst. for Soviet and East European Studies, John Carroll Univ., 1966. A bibliography of over 1,500 books on Eastern European countries, the Soviet Union, and world communism. Has a list of the most important periodicals for the study of communism.

Wiatr, Jerzy J., "Political Sociology in Eastern Europe; a trend report and bibliography," *Current Sociology,* Vol. XIII, No. 2, 1965. An annotated listing of 890 articles and books on political sociology published in the Soviet Union and Eastern European countries between 1957 and 1963.

U.S. Library of Congress. *Czechoslovakia; a bibliographic guide.* Rudolph Sturm, ed. Washington: Govt. Printing Off., 1967. Part I is a "Bibliographical Survey" describing and evaluating materials (primarily in English or Western European languages) useful for the study of Czechoslovakia. Has an eight-page section on "Politics and Government," plus similar sections on "Social Conditions," "Law" and related subjects. Part II is an alphabetical listing of over 1,500 publications discussed in Part I. The Library of Congress also has published three other bibliographic guides on East European countries, similar in format and coverage to the guide on Czechoslovakia, all with sections on politics, government, and foreign relations:

> *East Germany; a selected bibliography.* Arnold H. Price, ed. 1967. 833 items.

Bulgaria; a bibliographic guide. Marin V. Pundeff, ed. 1965. 1,248 items.

Rumania; a bibliographic guide. Stephen A. Fischer-Galati, ed. 1963. 748 items.

Sztaray, Zoltan. *Bibliography on Hungary.* New York: Kossuth Foundation, 1960. Unannotated listing of books not in Hungarian, including English. Has sections on "Political and Social Life," "International Relations," etc.

Halasz de Beky, I. L. *A Bibliography of the Hungarian Revolution, 1956.* Toronto: Univ. of Toronto Press, 1963. An unannotated listing of books and articles covering the period from October, 1956 to December, 1960. Arranged by language, with 928 English-language items cited. An appendix lists monitored broadcasts from Hungary and Russia during the revolution.

OTHER REFERENCE SOURCES

Florinsky, Michael T., ed. *McGraw-Hill Encyclopedia of Russia and the Soviet Union.* New York: McGraw-Hill, 1961. A general encyclopedia consisting of brief essays in a dictionary arrangement. Contains much biographical information, some brief bibliographies, and longer articles on government, international relations, the Communist party, and related subjects. The purpose is "to present, within the relatively brief space of a single volume, a mass of information on Russia before and after the revolution of 1917." For the political science student its primary utility will be as an introduction for the beginner and a reference source on dates, events, and people for the specialist.

Maxwell, Robert, ed. *Information USSR; an authoritative encyclopedia about the Union of Soviet Socialist Republics.* New York: Pergamon Press, 1962. Essentially an English-language version, with some revision, of Volume 50 of the *Bol'shaia Sovetskaia Entsiklopediia,* the official Soviet handbook on the USSR. This volume was part of the 1957 edition of the Soviet encyclopedia and can no longer be considered "authoritative."

Current Soviet Policies; the documentary record of the Communist Party Congress. New York: Columbia Univ. Press, 1952– . A series of volumes containing translations of the public proceedings of the CPSU

Congresses, beginning with the 19th Congress in 1952. A very useful compilation of material on each party congress which appeared in the weekly issues of the *Current Digest of the Soviet Press*. Contains texts of resolutions passed and officials elected by each congress.

Taafe, Robert H. *An Atlas of Soviet Affairs*. New York: Praeger, 1965. Brief descriptive coverage of political, economic, geographic and other aspects, with maps.

U.S. Department of State. *Soviet World Outlook; a handbook of Communist Statements*. 3rd ed. Washington: Department of State, 1959. A handbook of major statements by Communist leaders from Marx to Khrushchev, arranged by broad subject with a detailed index. A sort of "cold war catechism" of bad utterances from the other side.

Who's Who in the USSR, 1965/66. 2nd ed. New York: Scarecrow Press, 1966. "A biographical directory containing about 5,000 biographies of prominent personalities in the Soviet Union, compiled by the Institute for the Study of the USSR, Munich, Germany." Kept up-to-date by a quarterly supplement entitled *Portraits of Prominent USSR Personalities*.

Who's Who in Soviet Social Sciences, Humanities, Art, and Government. New York: Telberg Book Co., 1961. Biographical information on about 700 leading people. Based on a Soviet source published between 1958 and 1961.

Staar, Richard F. *The Communist Regimes in Eastern Europe; an introduction*. Stanford, Calif.: The Hoover Inst., 1967. A handbook containing concise chapters on each country, summarizing party and government organization and structure, foreign and domestic affairs, etc. General chapters cover the Warsaw Pact and CEMA. Has a bibliographical appendix.

ASIA AND CHINA

BIBLIOGRAPHIES

NOTE: See bibliographies in the "General Sources" section (this chapter) which deal with the British Empire, the Commonwealth and the British Colonial Office.

Bibliography of Asian Studies. Ann Arbor, Mich.: Assn. for Asian Studies, 1956–   . This annual bibliography appears as a special issue of the *Journal of Asian Studies* and consists of a listing of books and articles on Asia in general and on specific countries in the area. For each country there are separate sections on politics, foreign relations, and related subjects. The most comprehensive current bibliography available. From 1936 through 1955 appeared under the title "Far Eastern Bibliography" in the *Far Eastern Quarterly.* Cumulated author and subject catalogs of the "Bibliography of Asian Studies," covering the years 1941–1965, are scheduled to be published in October, 1969, by the G. K. Hall Company.

Library Catalogue of the School of Oriental and African Studies, University of London. 28 vs. Boston: G. K. Hall, 1963. These volumes are photographic reproductions of the card catalog of the School of Oriental and African Studies, which has one of the best library collections in these areas. Supplements going beyond 1963 are planned.

London. University. School of Oriental and African Studies. Library. *Monthly List of Periodical Articles on the Far East and South East Asia, 1954–65.* An author and subject listing of articles in periodicals on Asian affairs; the monthly lists were cumulated into an annual volume entitled *Far East and Southeast Asia; a cumulated list of periodical articles.* Ceased publication with No. 129, 1965.

U.S. Department of State. Bureau of Intelligence and Research. Office of External Research. *External Research: Asia.* Washington: Department of State, 1952–   . An annual listing of research in progress by academic specialists; listing is by country and subject, with sections on "Politics and Government," "Foreign Relations," etc. In 1964, separate lists on East Asia, South Asia, and Southeast Asia were merged into a general list on Asia.

Pearson, J. D. *Oriental and Asian Bibliography; an introduction with some reference to Africa.* Hamden, Conn.: Archon Books, 1966. A guide to bibliographies, library collections, reference books and research on Asian studies, by the Librarian of the School of Oriental and African Studies of London University. General coverage, but of some use to the advanced student.

Stucki, Curtis W. *American Doctoral Dissertations on Asia, 1933–1958.* Ithaca, N.Y.: Cornell Univ. Southeast Asia Program, Data Paper No.

37, 1959. An unannotated list of dissertations, arranged by country and subject. May be supplemented and updated by using *Dissertation Abstracts,* described in Chapter 11.

Bloomfield, B. C. *Theses on Asia Accepted by Universities in the United Kingdom and Ireland, 1877–1964.* London: Frank Cass & Co., 1967. Unannotated list of 2,500 theses and dissertations, arranged by country with subject sections.

Embree, Ainslie T., et al. *Asia; a guide to paperbacks.* rev. ed. New York: Asia Society, 1968. An annotated list of several hundred paperback books on the various regions of Asia in print as of late 1967. Embree's *Asia; a guide to basic books* (Asia Society, 1966) lists about 300 of the most important hardbound books on this area.

Taylor, C. R. H. *A Pacific Bibliography.* 2nd ed. New York: Oxford Univ. Press, 1965. Covers material "relating to the native peoples of Polynesia, Melanesia, and Micronesia." Lists 16,000 books and articles, with the emphasis on Anthropology.

Berton, Peter and Eugene Wu. *Contemporary China; a research guide.* Stanford, Calif.: Hoover Inst., 1967. (Hoover Inst. Bibliographical Series, No. 31.) "The purpose of this guide is to facilitate research on contemporary China by providing descriptions of the most significant bibliographical and reference works, selected documentary compilations, and listings of series, dissertations and theses." Lists over 2,200 items, many with extensive annotations. Emphasis is on materials in the social sciences and humanities, including both English-language and Chinese sources. Coverage is of post-1949 mainland China and post-1945 Taiwan. Excellent coverage of sources relating to the domestic and foreign affairs of both countries. The best starting point for any serious research on modern China or Taiwan.

U.S. Department of the Army. Library. *Communist China; a strategic survey, a bibliography.* Washington: Govt. Printing Off., 1966. Contains extensive annotations of about 650 books, articles, and documents on "the economic, sociological, military, and political fabric of Communist China." Updates *Communist China: Ruthless Enemy or Paper Tiger; a bibliographic survey,* issued by the Army Library in 1962.

Hucker, Charles O. *China; a critical bibliography*. Tucson: Univ. of Arizona Press, 1962. "A selected, graded, annotated list of books, articles, and individual chapters or sections of books that contribute significantly to the academic study of both traditional and modern China." Emphasis is on material in English published since 1940.

Lust, John. *Index Sinicus; a catalogue of articles relating to China in periodicals and other collective publications, 1920–1955*. Cambridge, Eng.: W. Heffer & Sons, 1964. Lists over 19,000 articles and essays, both scholarly and popular, in several hundred periodicals. Covers all subject fields but has sections on "Politics and Government," "Foreign Relations," etc.

Yuan, Tung-li. *China in Western Literature; a continuation of Cordier's Bibliotheca Sinica*. New Haven: Yale Univ. Far Eastern Publications, 1958. A comprehensive list of books published in English, French and German on China between 1921 and 1957. Covers all subjects, with sections on "Politics and Government," "Foreign Relations" and "Law and Legislation." Henri Cordier's *Bibliotheca Sinica* (Paris: Guilmoto, 1904–08) lists Western-language books and articles on China published prior to the 1920's and thus supplements the Lust and Yuan bibliographies.

Sorich, Richard. *Contemporary China; a bibliography of reports on China published by the U.S. Joint Publications Research Service*. New York: Readex Microprint Corporation, 1961. A list of JPRS translations issued from 1957 through July, 1960, with a subject index. See Chapter 9 of this guide for information on how to locate later JPRS translations on China.

Chen, Nai-Ruenn. *The Economy of Mainland China, 1949–1963; a bibliography of materials in English*. New York: Social Science Research Council, 1963. An unannotated list of books, documents, and articles, chiefly translations from Chinese sources. Intended primarily for economists, but there is some material of political science interest.

Cole, Allan B. *Forty Years of Chinese Communism; selected readings with commentary*. Washington: American Historical Assn. Service Center for Teachers of History, 1962. Analysis of developments and major publications relating to Chinese Communism since the early 1920's.

Rhoads, Edward J. M. *The Chinese Red Army, 1927–1963; an annotated bibliography*. Cambridge: Harvard Univ. Press, 1964. Lists about 600 writings on the Chinese Red Army from its beginnings in the 1927 Nanchang uprising to 1963. Attempts to list all important English-language writings, with selections of Chinese sources.

Rabe, Valentin H. *American-Chinese Relations, 1784–1941; books and pamphlets extracted from the shelflists of Widener Library*. (Research Aids for American Far Eastern Policy Studies, No. 1). Cambridge: distributed by Harvard Univ. Press, 1960. An unannotated list of English-language books and pamphlets on the economic, cultural and political relationships between the U.S. and China. Emphasis is on historical materials. Designed for use at Harvard, but of some general utility. No. 3 in this series of Research Aids lists Chinese-language resources. See, Robert L. Irick, et al., *American-Chinese Relations, 1784–1941; a survey of Chinese-language materials at Harvard*. (Research Aids for American Far Eastern Policy Studies, No. 3. Cambridge: distributed by Harvard Univ. Press, 1960.)

Harvard University. Library. *China, Japan, and Korea*. (Widener Library Shelflist, No. 14). Cambridge: Harvard Univ. Press, 1968. A classified list, with author and title indexes, of books on these countries in the Harvard Library.

U.S. Library of Congress. *Southeast Asia; an annotated bibliography of selected reference sources in Western languages*. rev. ed. Washington: Govt. Printing Off., 1964. Lists over 500 books and articles, with long annotations.

Southern Asia Social Science Bibliography. New Delhi: Unesco Research Centre on Social and Economic Development in Southern Asia, 1952– . An annual list, with annotations and abstracts, of social science books and articles in English published in India, Pakistan, the Philippines and other countries in the region south of China. Has a section on political science, with sub-sections on public administration and international relations. Prior to 1959, appeared as two separate publications, *South Asia Social Science Abstracts* and *South Asia Social Science Bibliography*.

Harvard University. Library. *Southern Asia*. (Widener Library Shelflist, No. 19). Cambridge: Harvard Univ. Press, 1968. A classified listing of books in the Harvard Library on India, Pakistan, Vietnam, Burma and other countries of South and Southeast Asia.

Hay, Stephen and Margaret H. Case. *Southeast Asian History; a bibliographic guide.* New York: Praeger, 1962. An annotated bibliography of books and articles, primarily in English, on the history of countries in Southeast Asia.

Embree, John F. *Bibliography of the Peoples and Cultures of Mainland Southeast Asia.* New Haven: Yale Univ. Southeast Asian Studies, 1950. An extensive listing of books and articles on all countries of the area, but oriented toward anthropology.

Berton, Peter and Alvin Z. Rubinstein. *Soviet Works on Southeast Asia; a bibliography of non-periodical literature, 1946–1965.* Los Angeles: Univ. of Southern California Press, 1967. Lists, by country and subject, about 400 Soviet books on Southeast Asia. The Introduction discusses Soviet periodicals relating to Southeast Asia.

NOTE: All of the bibliographies on Vietnam listed below are out-dated. The student researching the recent political or military situations there, or the American involvement, will have to "dig out" his sources from the indexes and abstracts discussed in Chapter 3 of this guide.

Keyes, Jane Godfrey. *Bibliography of Western Language Publications Concerning North Vietnam in the Cornell University Library.* Ithaca, N.Y.: Cornell Univ. Southeast Asia Program Data Paper No. 63, 1966. The Cornell Library has an extensive collection of material on Vietnam, however, and this bibliography lists its holdings, both of books and articles, on North Vietnam as of 1966. Has sections on "Politics and Government" and "Foreign Relations"; also lists all JPRS translations on North Vietnam. This bibliography supplements Data Paper No. 47, *A Bibliography of North Vietnam Publications in the Cornell University Library, September 1962.*

Coates, Joseph. *Bibliography of Vietnam.* Washington: Inst. for Defense Analyses, 1964. An unannotated listing of over 700 books and articles in English on both Vietnams. Has sections on "Government and Politics," "Public Administration," and "International Relations."

U.S. Department of State. Foreign Service Inst. Center for Area and Country Studies. *Viet-Nam; a selected bibliography.* Washington: Department of State, 1967. An unannotated listing, arranged by broad subject, of about 200 books and documents, mainly in English, on Vietnam.

U.S. Department of State. Bureau of Intelligence and Research. Office of External Research. *Democratic Republic of Viet-Nam (North Vietnam); a bibliography* and *Republic of Vietnam (South Vietnam); a bibliography*. Washington: Department of State, 1963. These companion bibliographies contain selected and annotated lists of writings, chiefly English and French, with some emphasis on political and military matters from 1945 to 1963.

Jumper, Roy. *Bibliography of the Political and Administrative History of Vietnam, 1802–1962*. Saigon: Michigan State Univ. Vietnam Advisory Group, 1962. Presumably, this was one of the less controversial products of the MSU group in Vietnam. An annotated listing of over 900 books and articles.

Michigan State University. Vietnam Project. *What to Read on Vietnam; a selected annotated bibliography*. 2nd ed. New York: Inst. of Pacific Relations, 1960. Lists books and articles, mainly in English, published from 1955 through October, 1959. Includes a list of periodicals published in Vietnam.

U.S. Library of Congress. *Indochina; a bibliography of the land and people*. Washington: Govt. Printing Off., 1950. Provides retrospective coverage of writings on Vietnam and other countries of former French Indochina. Covers all subjects, with sections on political topics. Emphasis is on writings published after 1930.

Bibliography of Material About Thailand in Western Languages. Bangkok: Chulalongkorn Univ. Lib., 1960. Unannotated list of books and articles, with an 18-page section on politics and government.

New York University. Burma Research Project. *Annotated Bibliography of Burma*. New Haven: Human Relations Area Files, 1956. Includes books, pamphlets, and articles, with sections on "Government," "Pre- and Post-War Politics," and "Foreign Relations."

U.S. Department of the Army. Library. *South Asia; a strategic survey*. Washington: Govt. Printing Off., 1966. Lists 750 writings with extensive annotations, on political, military, and economic factors in India, Pakistan, Afghanistan, and other countries in the area.

Chicago. University. College. *Introduction to the Civilization of India, South Asia; an introductory bibliography.* Chicago: Univ. of Chicago Press, 1962. A listing of over 4,000 writings, chiefly in English, on India, Pakistan, Nepal and Ceylon. Has a section on "Political and Economic Structure."

Case, Margaret H. *South Asian History, 1750–1950; a guide to periodicals, dissertations, and newspapers.* Princeton, N.J.: Princeton Univ. Press, 1968. A listing of over 6,000 articles and dissertations "on the history of the India-Pakistan subcontinent during the past two centuries." Parts I and II list articles and dissertations separately, covering all subjects, with sections on "Nationalism" and "Politics." Part II is a list of newspapers published in the area, with notations showing holdings of American libraries.

Nunn, G. Raymond. *South and Southeast Asia; a bibliography of bibliographies.* Honolulu: East-West Center, Univ. of Hawaii, 1966 (Occasional Papers, No. 4). Lists 350 bibliographies, which in turn list English and original-language sources, on the countries of Southern Asia.

Nunn, G. Raymond. *East Asia; a bibliography of bibliographies.* Honolulu: East-West Center, Univ. of Hawaii, 1967. (Occasional Papers, No. 7). A companion volume to the one above, listing bibliographies on East Asia, in general, and on China, Japan, Korea and Mongolia, specifically.

Guide to Indian Periodical Literature. Gurgaon (Harijana), India: Prabhu Book Service, 1964– . A quarterly subject and author index to articles appearing in about 150 periodicals (chiefly English-language) published in India. A general index covering all subjects but including political science.

Mahar, J. Michael. *India; a critical bibliography.* Tucson: Univ. of Arizona Press, 1964. An annotated bibliography on all subjects, chiefly of books published since 1940.

Wilson, Patrick. *Government and Politics of India and Pakistan, 1885–1955; a bibliography of works in Western languages.* Berkeley: Inst.

of East Asiatic Studies, Univ. of California, 1956. An extensive, but unannotated, listing of books, articles, and other sources. Has sections on "Political Parties," "Government and Administration" and "International Relations."

Gautam, Brijenda Pratap. *Researches in Political Science in India; a detailed bibliography*. Kanpur, India: Oriental Publishing House, 1965. An unannotated listing of dissertations and theses completed in Indian universities on political science subjects. Listed first by university, then by broad subject areas.

Sarkar, Bidyut Kumar. *A Selected and Annotated Bibliography of the Government, Politics, and Foreign Relations of India*. Berkeley: South Asia Project, Univ. of California, 1956. Much more selective than the Wilson bibliography listed above, but with annotations.

Sharma, Jagdish. *Indian National Congress; a descriptive bibliography of India's struggle for freedom*. Delhi: S. Chand, 1959. An extensive bibliography, with some annotations, of "all literature available regarding the activities of the Indian National Congress since its inception."

Cohn, Bernard S. *The Development and Impact of British Administration in India; a bibliographic essay*. New Delhi: Indian Inst. of Public Admin., 1961. A review and analysis of English-language writing relating to British public administration in India.

Ali, Shaukat and Richard W. Gable. *Pakistan; a selected bibliography*. Los Angeles: Intl. Public Admin. Center, Sch. of Public Admin., Univ. of Southern California, 1966. An unannotated bibliography of about 500 writings in English on "the formation of Pakistan, the influence of Islam, constitutional development, government, politics, administration, and the various aspects of national development."

Maron, Stanley, et al. *Annotated Bibliography for Pakistan; sociology, economics, and politics*. Berkeley: South Asia Project, Univ. of California, 1956. Has a 19-page section on politics. A revised edition of this bibliography, edited by Donald Wilber, is scheduled to be published shortly.

National Book Centre of Pakistan. *Books on Pakistan; a bibliography*. 2nd ed. Karachi: National Book Centre, 1965. Unannotated list of books on Pakistan, chiefly in English. Has brief sections on "Foreign Relations," "Constitutional Studies," and "Administration and Basic Democracy."

Abernathy, George L. *Pakistan: a selected, annotated bibliography.* 2nd rev. ed. New York: American Inst. of Pacific Relations, 1960. An annotated listing of books, Pakistani government documents, and periodical articles.

Wilber, Donald N. *Annotated Bibliography of Afghanistan.* 3rd ed. New Haven: Human Relations Area Files, 1968. A classified listing of over 1,200 books and articles, chiefly in Western languages.

An Annotated Bibliography of Philippine Social Sciences. Quezon City: Social Science Research Center, Univ. of the Philippines, 1956– . Three volumes have been issued to date, on economics, sociology, and political science. Vol. 3, pt. 1 on "Political Science" appeared in 1960 and is an annotated bibliography of over 1,300 books, articles, and documents on all aspects of political science in the Philippines.

Index to Philippine Periodicals. Manila: Inter-Departmental Reference Service, Inst. of Public Admin., Univ. of the Philippines, 1956– . A semiannual subject and author index to articles in about 100 journals published in the Philippines. Covers all subjects, including political science and public administration.

Ward, Robert E. and Jajime Watanabe. *Japanese Political Science; a guide to Japanese reference and research materials.* Ann Arbor: Center for Japanese Studies, Univ. of Michigan, 1961. Descriptive bibliography of books, articles and reference works, with sections on "Political Parties," "Elections," and related subjects. Chiefly Japanese-language sources.

Webb, Herschel. *Research in Japanese Sources; a guide.* New York: Columbia Univ. Press, 1965. "A beginner's guide to the subject of Japanese bibliography." Mentions major English-language sources but primarily for the student who can read Japanese.

American Library Association. *Guide to Japanese Reference Books.* Chicago: ALA, 1966. A bibliography of Japanese-language bibliographies and other reference books on all subjects, with a section on

"Political Science." Titles are transliterated, and annotations are in English.

A Classified List of Books in Western Languages Relating to Japan. Tokyo: Univ. of Tokyo Press, 1966. A subject listing of books in the library of the Society for International Cultural Relations. Has sections on "Politics" and "National Defense."

Borton, Hugh. *A Selected List of Books and Articles on Japan in English, French and German.* rev. ed. Cambridge: Harvard Univ. Press, 1954. Annotated list of about 1,800 books and articles; sections on "Government and Politics," "World War II," and the "Occupation."

Silberman, Bernard S. *Japan and Korea; a critical bibliography.* Tucson: Univ. of Arizona Press, 1962. "Selected, annotated and graded guide to the most authoritative works on Japan and Korea." Chiefly recent English-language material. Over 1,900 books and articles, with sections on "Political Patterns," "History" and "Social Organization and Structure."

Hazard, B. H., et al. *Korean Studies Guide.* Berkeley: Univ. of California Press, 1954. Purpose is "to provide a handbook of basic information necessary to pursuing the study of the various aspects of Korean culture." Refers chiefly to Korean sources, with a 19-page section of "Government, Economics, and Recent History."

Yong-sun Chung. *Korea; a selected bibliography, 1959–1963.* Seoul: The Korean Research and Pubns., Inc., 1965. Unannotated list of 167 books and articles in English and Korean. Earlier coverage is provided by Sun-hi Yi, *Korea: a selected bibliography in Western languages, 1950–1958* (Berkeley: Univ. of California Press, 1959).

Blanchard, Carroll H. *Korean War Bibliography and Maps of Korea.* Albany, N.Y.: Korean Conflict Research Foundation,1964. Aim is "to present a complete and accurate listing of sources of information on the Korean War." Subject listing of books and periodicals, primarily American and other Western sources.

OTHER REFERENCE SOURCES

Asian Recorder. New Delhi: M. H. Samuel, 1955– . A weekly loose-leaf news service summarizing material from Asian newspapers and other sources, with brief section on each country. Also covers several countries of the Middle East. There is a quarterly index which is cumulated annually.

Wint, Guy. *Asia; a handbook*. New York: Praeger, 1966. An encyclopedic handbook covering all Asian countries. Part I on "Basic Information" contains summary statistical data; Part II has brief essays on each country by specialists; Part III has articles on general topics, including a section on "Political Affairs"; Part IV contains the texts of treaties and agreements relating to Asia. Each article has a brief, selected bibliography.

Asian Annual; the "Eastern World" handbook. London: Eastern World, 1954– . Contains brief descriptive and statistical information on each country. Has a section on diplomatic representation listing embassies of Asian countries abroad and foreign representation in each country of Asia.

Asian Who's Who. 3rd ed. Hong Kong: Pan Asian Newspaper Alliance, 1960. Brief biographical sketches of leading personalities in all Asian countries.

Asia Society. *American Institutions and Organizations Interested in Asia*. 2nd ed. New York: Taplinger, 1961. Alphabetical list of about 1,000 organizations, with brief description of their programs relating to Asia.

Kirby, E. Stuart, ed. *Contemporary China*. Hong Kong: Univ. of Hong Kong Press, 1955– . An annual compendium of articles, documents, and an extensive chronology of developments in China. Each volume also has a selected bibliography listing mainly Chinese-language writings but with some English-language books and articles. Apparently ceased publication with Volume VI, 1962–63, but with similar coverage continued by *China Mainland Review,* 1965– , a quarterly journal published by the Institute of Modern Asian Studies, University of Hong Kong.

Communist China. Hong Kong: Union Research Inst., 1955– . A series of annual volumes summarizing developments in Communist China. Has sections on "Party Affairs," "Foreign Affairs," "Military Affairs," and other subjects. Issued by one of the many private research organizations or publishers in Hong Kong which specialize in "China watching." Somewhat similar to, but less authoritative than, the two sources listed above.

The Great Cultural Revolution in China. Hong Kong: Asia Research Centre, 1967. A collection of several hundred official documents and statements by Chinese leaders on the origin and development of the Cultural Revolution. Contains a glossary of terms and a chronology. A somewhat similar collection appears in K. H. Fan, *The Chinese Cultural Revolution; selected documents.* New York: Monthly Review Press, 1968.

Who's Who in Communist China. Hong Kong: Union Research Inst., 1966. Biographical information on 1,200 leading figures in Communist China.

U.S. Department of State. Bureau of Intelligence and Research. *Intelligence Research Aid: Directory of Chinese Communist Officials.* Washington: Department of State, 1966. "This directory of Chinese Communist officials identifies the leading Chinese political, governmental, and socio-cultural personalities." Has sections on party, central and provincial government officials, mass organizations, and the diplomatic corps. Lists officials as of February, 1966, before the shakeup resulting from the Great Proletarian Cultural Revolution.

U.S. Department of State. Bureau of Intelligence and Research. *Chinese Communist World Outlook; a handbook of Chinese Communist statements.* Washington: Govt. Printing Off., 1962. "Presents the chief motivating ideas and theories of the Chinese Communists in the words of the Chinese leaders themselves." Divided into sections on "Ideology and Ideological Problems," "Domestic Problems and Policies," and "Foreign Policy." A handy source for quotations, but certainly more than a random selection of statements.

U.S. Library of Congress. *Guide to Selected Legal Sources of Mainland China.* Washington: Govt. Printing Off., 1967. "A listing of laws and regulations and periodical legal literature with a brief survey of the administration of justice." Contains translated titles of laws and other legal documents for the 1949–1963 period and a bibliography of articles from legal and general periodicals published in Communist China.

Johnston, Douglas M. and Hungdah Chiu. *Agreements of the Peoples'
Republic of China, 1949–1967; a calendar.* Cambridge: Harvard Univ.
Press, 1968. A chronological listing of treaties and other agreements
engaged in by Communist China. Cites English-language versions
when available. The appendix lists agreements by country and subject.

Blaustein, Albert P., ed. *Fundamental Legal Documents of Communist
China.* South Hackensack, N.J.: Rothman, 1962. Translations of the
constitutions of the People's Republic and the Party, the Common
Program, and organic laws.

China Yearbook. Taipei: China Publishing Co., 1937/43– . A general
handbook on the political, social structure of Nationalist China, with
some statistical and biographical data. Published irregularly. Sections
on "Government and Its Functions," "National Defense," "International Affairs," etc. Contains texts of major laws and speeches by
Nationalist leaders.

Boorman, Howard L. *Biographical Directory of Republican China.* Vol. I.
New York: Columbia Univ. Press, 1967. Will run to several volumes
and contain biographical articles on Chinese who were prominent
during the period 1911–1949.

India; a reference annual. Delhi: Ministry of Information and Broadcasting, 1953– . A general handbook containing statistical and directory data, with summary information on political and other developments in the country. Sections on the "Constitution," "Legislature,"
"Executive," "Judiciary," "Defense," etc. Appendices contain some
election statistics and a selected bibliography.

Baranwal, S. P., ed. *Military Year Book.* New Delhi: Guide Pubns.,
1965– . An organizational handbook, directory, and summary of
activities of the Indian armed forces. Contains considerable information, from the Indian viewpoint, on hostilities with Pakistan and China.

Pakistan Press Index. Karachi: Documentation and Information Bureau,
Nadia House, 1966– . Unexamined, but apparently a digest and
summary of material in Pakistani newspapers.

Japanese National Commission for Unesco. *Japan; its land, people and
culture.* rev. ed. Tokyo: Ministry of Finance, 1964. An encyclopedia

of Japan covering all subjects. Has sections on "Government and Political Organization," "International Relations and Diplomacy."

Japan Biographical Encyclopedia and Who's Who, 1964–65. 3rd ed. Tokyo: Renzo Press, 1964. Biographical data on about 15,000 individuals.

Kai, Miwa and Philip Yampolsky. *Political Chronology of Japan, 1885–1957.* New York: East Asian Inst., Columbia Univ., 1957. Lists government and party leaders, legislators, and a chronology of politically significant events.

AFRICA AND THE MIDDLE EAST

BIBLIOGRAPHIES

NOTE: See bibliographies in the "General Sources" section (this chapter) which deal with the British Empire, the Commonwealth and the British Colonial Office.

U.S. Library of Congress. *Africa South of the Sahara; a selected, annotated list of writings.* Washington: Govt. Printing Off., 1963. An annotated bibliography of over 2,100 books and articles on all subjects. Good coverage of political science materials, with a general section on "Politics and Economics" and similar sub-sections under each country of sub-Saharan Africa. May be supplemented and updated through: Peter C. W. Gutkind and John B. Webster, *A Select Bibliography on Traditional and Modern Africa.* Syracuse, N.Y.: Program of Eastern African Studies, Syracuse Univ., 1968. This source lists about 3,000 books and articles in English published since 1962.

A Current Bibliography on African Affairs. New York: Greenwood Periodicals for the African Bibliographic Center of Washington, 1962– . "Compiled as a bimonthly guide for study and research in the field of African studies and related subjects." Each issue lists about 200 current books and articles; has a "General Subject" section with sub-sections on "Politics and Government" and "Foreign Relations" plus a geographical section which lists writings by country. The African Bibliographic Center also issues a "Special Bibliography Series" which consists of bibliographies of current writings on particular countries or topics. The *Current Bibliography* was published by the African Bibliographic Center from 1962 to August, 1967, when Greenwood Periodicals began to issue it in a new format. It is now the best current bibliographic source on Africa.

U.S. Department of the Army. *Africa: problems and prospects; a bibliographic survey*. Washington: Department of the Army, 1967. An annotated bibliography of over 900 books and articles which deal with the current problems of Africa and the "emerging economic, political, and social picture of the continent's prospects for the future." Has a section on each country plus a general section which includes political and military subjects. The Appendix includes a summary on "The Armed Forces of African States" plus detailed maps.

United States and Canadian Publications on Africa. Stanford, Calif.: The Hoover Inst., 1960–   . An annual listing of all books, pamphlets, and articles published in the U.S. and Canada on sub-Saharan Africa. Section I is entitled "Works on Africa by Topics" and has sub-sections on "Politics and Government" and "International Relations." Section II is on "Works Dealing with Specific Regions." Usually about two years behind, thus not a current source. The volume for 1960 was published by the Library of Congress; subsequent volumes have appeared as part of The Hoover Institution Bibliographical Series.

Hanna, William J. and Judith L. *Politics in Black Africa; a selective bibliography of relevant periodical literature*. East Lansing: African Studies Center, Michigan State Univ., 1964. An unannotated listing of over 1,200 periodical articles in English and French. Arranged by topic rather than by country, with emphasis on recent writing.

Alderfer, Harold F. *A Bibliography of African Government, 1950–1966*. 2nd ed. Lincoln, Pa.: Lincoln Univ. Press, 1967. An unannotated but extensive listing of several thousand books and periodical articles on government, politics, and public administration in Africa. Arranged by country, with an author but no subject index.

Lystad, Robert A. *The African World; a survey of social research*. New York: Praeger, 1965. Critical and analytical essays, by specialists, of research in various disciplines on Africa. Has a chapter on political science by Harvey Glickman, with a bibliography of major works.

African Bibliographic Center. *The Sword and Government; a preliminary and selected bibliographical guide to African military affairs*. Washington: African Bibliographic Center, 1967. (Special Bibliographic Series, Vol. 5, No. 2.) A two-part bibliography of books and articles on African military affairs.

U.S. Library of Congress. *Serials for African Studies.* Washington: Govt. Printing Off., 1961. A list of about 2,000 periodicals, annuals, etc., published in Africa and elsewhere which are of value for African studies. A revised edition is scheduled to be published shortly.

U.S. Library of Congress. *African Newspapers in Selected American Libraries.* 3rd ed. Washington: Govt. Printing Off., 1965. A union list of the "current and retrospective holdings of African newspapers in 33 selected libraries."

Catalog of the African Collection of the Northwestern University Library. Boston: G. K. Hall, 1963. Reproduces in book form the card catalog of Northwestern's African collection, which emphasizes sub-Saharan Africa.

Joint Acquisitions List of Africana. Evanston, Ill.: Northwestern Univ. Lib., 1962– . A union list of materials published in or on Africa received by Northwestern, the Library of Congress, Boston University, and other libraries with strong African collections. Will be of primary value as a research and interlibrary loan tool for the advanced student.

Catalog of African Government Documents and African Area Index, Boston University Libraries. 2nd ed. Boston: G. K. Hall, 1964. Lists about 4,000 official publications of the various African states held by the Boston University Library.

Harvard University. Library. *Africa.* Cambridge: Harvard Univ. Press, 1965. (Widener Library Shelflist, No. 2.) A list of books on Africa in the Harvard Library, with separate listings by author, classification number, and date of publication.

U.S. Department of State. Bureau of Intelligence and Research. Office of External Research. *External Research: Africa.* Washington: Department of State, 1953– . An annual listing of research in progress by American scholars and research centers, with sections on politics, government and international relations.

Bulletin of Information on Current Research on Human Sciences Concerning Africa. Brussels: Intl. Centre for African Economic and Social

Documentation, 1963– . Attempts to list research in progress on a worldwide basis. Has sections on "Political Science" and "Public Administration." Annotations are in English and French.

U.S. Library of Congress. *A List of American Doctoral Dissertations on Africa.* Washington: Govt. Printing Off., 1962. An unannotated listing, by author, of about 700 dissertations accepted by American universities from the late 19th century to 1960–61. May be supplemented and updated by *Dissertation Abstracts,* described in Chapter 11 of this guide.

Rosenblum, Paul. *Checklist of Paperbound Books on Africa.* New York: Foreign Area Materials Center, Univ. of the State of New York, 1965. A list of paperback books in print as of September, 1965. May be kept up to date through *Paperbound Books in Print.*

African Bibliographic Center. *African Affairs for the General Reader; a selected introductory bibliographical guide, 1960–1967.* New York: Council of the African-American Inst., 1967. Lists and describes 1,700 periodicals, books and articles on Africa. Designed for the nonspecialist but will serve as a resource for the student who is beginning to study Africa.

Holdsworth, Mary. *Soviet African Studies, 1918–1959.* New York: Oxford Univ. Press, 1961. A two-part bibliography prepared for the Royal Institute of International Affairs. Lists and annotates books and articles on Africa published in the Soviet Union. Part I, on "General Functional Studies," contains a section on "Politics." Part II, "Regional Studies," is arranged by area. Also see Ladislav Venya, *A Select Bibliography of Soviet Publications on Africa in General and Eastern Africa in Particular, 1962–1966.* Syracuse, N.Y.: Program of Eastern African Studies, Syracuse Univ., 1968.

Central Asian Research Centre, London. *Soviet Writing on Africa, 1959–1961; an annotated bibliography.* London: Oxford Univ. Press, 1963. A supplement to Holdsworth, listing writings from 1959 through 1961, plus some omitted from the earlier bibliography.

Simms, Ruth P. *Urbanization in West Africa; a review of current literature.* Evanston, Ill.: Northwestern Univ. Press, 1965. An annotated bibliography of about 300 books and articles published from 1950 to

1964, chiefly on the social and political aspects of urbanization in West Africa.

Johnson, A. F. *A Bibliography of Ghana, 1930–1961.* Evanston, Ill.: Northwestern Univ. Press, 1964. Attempts to list all books on Ghana and the Gold Coast published during these years, with some periodical articles. Has a section on "Politics and Government." May be updated by "A Bibliography of Ghana, 1958–1964," in the September, 1967, issue of *African Studies Bulletin.*

Dipeolu, J. O. *Bibliographical Sources for Nigerian Studies.* Evanston, Ill.: Program of African Studies, Northwestern Univ., 1966. A brief, annotated bibliography including a section on "History, Politics and Government," which lists about 30 sources.

Solomon, Marvin D. *A General Bibliography of the Republic of Liberia.* Evanston, Ill.: Northwestern Univ. African Program, 1962. An unannotated listing of about a thousand books, articles, and documents on Liberia. Arranged by author or type of material, with no subject index. Intended as a preliminary version of an enlarged edition, which has not yet appeared.

U.S. Department of State. Bureau of Intelligence and Research. Office of External Research. *Kenya, Uganda, Tanganyika; a bibliography.* Washington: Department of State, 1964. Lists writings on these countries published from 1960 to February, 1964. Has sections on "Politics" and "Political Development."

Webster, John B. *A Bibliography on Kenya.* Syracuse, N.Y.: Program of Eastern African Studies, Syracuse Univ., 1967. An unannotated but comprehensive listing of over 7,200 articles, books and other writings on Kenya. Covers all subjects, with 732 items on "Politics and Government." Author and subject indexes.

Kuria, Lucas, et al. *A Bibliography on Politics and Government in Uganda.* Syracuse, N.Y.: Bibliographic Section, Program of Eastern African Studies, Syracuse Univ., 1965. (Occasional Bibliography No. 2.) Unannotated listing of about 300 articles, books, and official publications. Arranged alphabetically by author with no subject index.

Brown, Edward E., et al. *A Bibliography of Malawi. Syracuse, N.Y.:* Syracuse Univ. Press, 1965. An attempt at a complete but unannotated bibliography of all writings on Malawi and Nyasaland. Has a 20-page section on "Government and Politics."

Matthews, Daniel G. *A Current Bibliography on Ethiopian Affairs.* Washington: African Bibliographic Center, 1965. (Special Bibliographic Series, Vol. 3, No. 3.) Unannotated listing of several hundred books and articles published during the years 1950–1964 on Ethiopia. Supplemented by *Ethiopian Panorama: a select bibliographical survey, 1965–1966.* (Special Bibliographic Series, Vol. 5, No. 1.)

Nasri, Abdel Rahman. *A Bibliography of the Sudan, 1938–1958.* New York: Oxford Univ. Press, 1962. Unannotated list of books and articles, with a section on "Government and Politics." May be updated by Daniel G. Matthews, *A Current Bibliography on Sudanese Affairs, 1960–1964* (Washington: African Bibliographic Center, 1965. Special Bibliographic Series, Vol. 3, No. 4.)

Africana Nova. Capetown: South African Public Lib., 1958– . "A quarterly bibliography of books currently published in and about the Republic of South Africa."

Middle East Journal. Washington: Middle East Inst., 1947– . Each quarterly issue has a "Bibliography of Periodical Literature" which carries a "selective listing of periodical material dealing with the Middle East since the rise of Islam." Has a section on "Modern History and Politics."

U.S. Department of the Army. Library. *Middle East; Tricontinental Hub, a strategic survey.* Washington: Govt. Printing Off., 1965. An annotated bibliography of books, articles, and documents relating to the "military, political, economic, and sociological aspects" of the Middle East. Sections on each country, plus a general section on "Strategic Implications of the Environment." Appendices contain statistical data and a list of reference sources.

Middle East Social Science Bibliography: Arab countries of the Middle East, 1955–1960. Cairo: Unesco Middle East Science Cooperation Off., 1961. An unannotated listing of books and articles published in the Arabic-speaking countries of the Middle East. Refers primarily to Arabic-language sources but lists some English-language works. An earlier volume, published by the Middle East Science Cooperation Office in 1959, covers the years 1945–1955.

Pearson, J. D. *Index Islamicus, 1906–1955; a catalogue of articles on Islamic subjects in periodicals and other collective publications.* Cambridge, Eng.: W. Heffer, 1958. A classified listing, without annotations, of over 26,000 articles and essays. Covers all fields, and not particularly strong in the social sciences, but useful for historical coverage. Two supplements have been issued, bringing coverage up through 1965.

A Selected Bibliography of Articles Dealing with the Middle East. Jerusalem: Economic Research Inst., Hebrew Univ. Unannotated listing of articles appearing in about 30 journals, with sections on "Politics and Government," "Society," etc. Published in two volumes covering the years 1939–1950 and 1951–1954.

U.S. Library of Congress. *North and Northwest Africa; a selected, annotated list of writings, 1951–1957.* Washington: Govt. Printing Off., 1957. Annotated bibliography of about 400 books and documents on the countries along the southern Mediterranean coast. Emphasis on social, economic, and political aspects.

Ettinghausen, Richard. *A Selected and Annotated Bibliography of Books and Periodicals in Western Languages Dealing with the Near and Middle East.* Washington: Middle East Inst., 1954. Annotated listing of about 2,000 books and periodicals in Western languages. General coverage, with very little attention paid to political science material.

Ljunggren, Florence and Mohammed Hamdy. *Annotated Guide to Journals Dealing with the Middle East and North Africa.* Cairo: The American Univ. in Cairo Press, 1965. Lists about 300 journals, Arabic and Western, with a subject index indicating those relating to political science.

U.S. Department of State. Bureau of Intelligence and Research. Office of External Research. *External Research: Middle East.* Washington: Department of State, 1953– . An annual listing of research in progress by American academic specialists, with sections on "Politics and Government" and "International Relations."

Bolton, A. R. C. *Soviet Middle East Studies; an analysis and bibliography.* New York: Oxford Univ. Press, 1959. An eight-part listing and analysis of Soviet writing on the Arab world. See *Mizan* (Chapter 9 of this guide) for continuing coverage in English of Soviet writing on the Middle East.

OTHER REFERENCE SOURCES

Africa Research Bulletin. Exeter, Eng.: Africa Research Ltd., 1964– . A digest of press articles and other sources on current events in Africa. Issued in two parts: "Political, Social and Cultural Series" and "Economic, Financial and Technical Series." Each series is published monthly with quarterly cumulative indexes.

African Recorder. New Delhi: M. N. Samuel, 1962– . A fortnightly news digest, summarizing and quoting from major newspapers. Arrangement is by country, with a separate section on "Africa outside Africa" which summarizes news from European, American and other sources outside Africa.

Legum, Colin, ed. *Africa; a handbook to the continent.* Rev. and enl. ed. New York: Praeger, 1966. Part I has separate articles on each country, written by specialists, containing descriptive and historical material. Part II has sections on culture, religion and economics of the continent as a whole, plus a section on attitudes toward Africa in Europe, the U.S. and Russia. Each article has some summary statistical data and brief bibliographies. Probably the best of the handbooks on Africa.

Kitchen, Helen, ed. *A Handbook of African Affairs.* New York: Praeger, 1964. Part I consists of brief, three-to-four page "political guides" on each country in Africa. Part II is on "The Armies of Africa," with brief summaries and statistical data. Part III is on "The Organization of African Unity." Based on material which appeared originally in the monthly periodical, *African Report.*

Junod, Violaine I. *The Handbook of Africa.* New York: New York Univ. Press, 1963. Brief descriptive and statistical data on each country, designed to provide "comparable factual information on each of the fifty-odd political units of Africa." Originally prepared as a handbook for use in a course for foreign-aid technicians.

Boyd, Andrew and Patrick von Rensburg. *An Atlas of African Affairs.* rev. ed. New York: Praeger, 1965. Contains general and sectional maps, with accompanying text, presenting summary information on the demographic, physical, economic and social conditions in African countries.

Segal, Ronald. *Political Africa; a who's who of personalities and parties.* London: Stevens & Sons, 1961. Brief biographies of leading political figures, plus sections on the political parties of each country, including information on their leadership, membership and recent political history.

In addition to the handbooks listed above, which were produced primarily by academic specialists with an emphasis on political aspects, there are several annuals, directories, and yearbooks—produced chiefly by commercial organizations or publishers—which contain descriptive data on African countries. Most of those listed below have directories of government officials plus sections on diplomatic representation:

> *Africa Annual.* London: Foreign Correspondents, Ltd., 1958– .
> *West African Directory.* London: Thomas Skinner & Co., 1962– .
> *West Africa Annual.* 2nd ed. Lagos, Nigeria: John West, Ltd., 1964–65.
> *Year Book and Guide to East Africa.* London: Robert Hale, Ltd., 1950– .
> *Year Book and Guide to Southern Africa.* London: Robert Hale, Ltd., 1893– .

Taylor, Sidney, ed. *The New Africans; a guide to the contemporary history of emergent Africa and its leaders.* New York: Putnam, 1967. Contains brief histories of each independent country of sub-Saharan Africa, plus biographies of about 600 contemporary political, military, governmental and other African leaders. Written by correspondents for Reuters news agency.

Duignan, Peter. *Handbook of American Resources for African Studies.* Stanford, Calif.: The Hoover Inst., 1967. (Hoover Inst. Bibliographical Series, No. 29.) A description of the library, archival and manuscript materials relevant to African studies in major American university and other libraries.

Unesco. *Social Scientists Specializing in African Studies.* Paris: Mouton, 1963. Brief biographical information on over 2,000 African specialists in the U.S. and elsewhere.

Mideast Mirror; a review of Middle East news. Beirut, Lebanon: Regional News Service, 1948– . A weekly summary of news developments in the Middle East, edited from news reports. Has a quarterly index which lists articles by country.

Arab Political Documents. Beirut: Political Studies and Public Admin. Department, American Univ. of Beirut, 1963– . An annual collection and translation of diplomatic and political documents, statements, and manifestoes of parties, pressure groups, political leaders, and other organizations in Arab countries.

Chronology of Arab Politics. Beirut: Political Studies and Public Admin. Department, American Univ. of Beirut, 1963– . A quarterly chronology of political developments, based on Arabic sources. Arranged by country with an annual index.

The Middle East and North Africa. London: Europa Publications, Ltd., 1948– . Part I is a "General Survey" containing articles on such special topics as "Oil in the Middle East," "The Arab League," etc. Part II has sections on each country, covering geography, history and economic factors, plus statistical data, directories of government officials, and brief bibliographies. Part III is a "Who's Who" section with biographical data on leaders in government, education, business and other fields.

Middle East Record. Tel Aviv: Israel Oriental Society, 1960– . "An annual account of the politics and international relations of the countries of the Middle East." An encyclopedic survey containing a descriptive chronology of events, official views of the various governments, etc. Several years behind in publishing, the volume for 1961 appeared in 1966.

Kingsbury, Robert and Norman Pounds. *An Atlas of Middle Eastern Affairs.* New York: Praeger, 1963. Maps and brief text on the economy, geography and politics of Middle Eastern countries. Emphasis is on geographic and physical factors.

Who's Who in Israel. Tel Aviv: Who's Who in the State of Israel Publishing House, 1945– . Directory of government officials, biographical sketches, and directory of private organizations.

Ljunggren, Florence and Charles Geddes. *An International Directory of Institutions and Societies Interested in the Middle East.* New York: Stechert-Hafner, 1962. A list of about 350 organizations which specialize in Middle Eastern affairs, with descriptions of their programs.

LATIN AMERICA

BIBLIOGRAPHIES

NOTE: See bibliographies in the "General Sources" section (this chapter) which deal with the British Empire, the Commonwealth and the British Colonial Office.

Sable, Martin H. *Guide to Latin American Studies.* 2 vs. Los Angeles: Latin American Center, Univ. of California at Los Angeles, 1967. An annotated bibliography of approximately 5,000 general and reference books relevant to the study of Latin America. Designed to "facilitate research at the undergraduate and graduate level in any discipline and/or professional field related to Latin America." Volume 2 has an extensive section on "Political Science," with sub-sections on "Elections," "Inter-American Affairs," "Political Parties," "Revolution," "U.S. Foreign Policy," and other topics. An excellent up-to-date source, one of the best starting points for study of Latin America.

Handbook of Latin American Studies. Gainesville, Fla.: Univ. of Florida Press, 1935– . Each annual volume, containing chapters produced by specialists, lists several thousand books and articles on Latin America. Covers all subject fields, with sections on "Government and International Relations," "History," "Sociology," etc. Primary arrangement is by subject, with secondary arrangement by country. Has author and subject indexes. Beginning with Vol. 26, 1964, each volume covers the Social Sciences and the Humanities in alternating years. An essential bibliographic source.

Latin American Research Review. Austin, Texas: Latin American Research Review Board, 1965– . A quarterly periodical "devoted to systematic reviewing of current studies of Latin America." Among other features, each issue has a "Current Research Inventory" which lists and describes research in progress in all fields of Latin American studies.

Gropp, Arthur E. *A Bibliography of Latin American Bibliographies.* Metuchen, N.J.: Scarecrow Press, 1968. A listing of some 7,200 bibliographies in all languages on Latin America, arranged by subject, then by country. Has sections on "Political Science," "International Relations," and "Public Administration." This is an updating of the second (1942) edition of this work, compiled by C. K. Jones.

U.S. Department of State. Bureau of Intelligence and Research. Office of External Research. *External Research: American Republics.* Washington: Department of State, 1953– . An annual listing of research in progress by American academic specialists, with sections on "Politics and Government" and "International Relations."

Trask, David F., et al. *A Bibliography of United States-Latin American Relations Since 1810.* Lincoln: Univ. of Nebraska Press, 1968. A listing, with some annotations, of over 11,000 books, articles and other sources on U.S. relations with Latin America. Chapters are arranged chronologically and by country. Covers works in all languages and is easily the most comprehensive bibliography on the subject.

U.S. Department of the Army. *Latin America; hemispheric partner; a bibliographic survey.* Washington: Govt. Printing Off., 1964. An annotated listing of several hundred books and articles "reflective of the strategic, political, economic and sociological aspects as they apply both to the external and internal image of Latin America." Primarily English-language sources.

Caribbean Studies. San Juan: Inst. of Caribbean Studies, Univ. of Puerto Rico, 1961– . Each issue of this quarterly journal carries an extensive "Current Bibliography" section listing, without annotations, all known books and periodical articles on countries in Central America and the Caribbean. Arranged by country, with separate book and article sections, but without a subject index.

Bayitch, S. A. *Latin America and the Caribbean; a bibliographical guide to works in English.* Coral Gables, Fla.: Univ. of Miami Press, 1967. A very extensive, unannotated, bibliography of several thousand books and articles. Arrangement is by country and subject, with sections on "Politics," "Foreign Relations," "Government," "Elections," etc. A revision of the author's *Latin America; a bibliographic guide* (1961) which was limited largely to legal materials.

Comitas, Lambros. *Caribbeana 1900–1965; a topical bibliography.* Seattle, Wash: Univ. of Washington Press, 1968. An unannotated bibliography of over 7,000 writings on the non-Hispanic Caribbean region published in the twentieth century. Covers all subjects, but with emphasis on social science materials, and has a 56-page section on "Political Issues." Since this does not include Latin America or the Hispanic Caribbean, the coverage is much more specialized than Bayitch.

U.S. Library of Congress. Hispanic Foundation. *Latin America; an annotated bibliography of paperback books.* Washington: Govt. Printing Off., 1967. (Hispanic Foundation Bibliographic Series, No. 11.) Annotated listing of over 600 recent paperbacks on Latin America, arranged by author with a subject index. May be kept up-to-date through *Paperbound Books in Print.*

Canning House Library. 5 vs. Boston: G. K. Hall, 1967. An author and subject catalog of the holdings of the Canning House Library in London. This library specializes in coverage of Latin America, Spain, and Portugal. The catalog reproduces about 48,000 cards representing over 20,000 books, with emphasis on Latin America.

Grossman, Jorge. *Bibliography on Public Administration in Latin America.* 2nd ed. Washington: Pan American Union, 1958. Unannotated listing of over 3,000 books and articles. Refers primarily to Spanish-language sources.

Kantor, Harry. *Latin American Political Parties; a bibliography.* Gainesville, Fla.: Univ. of Florida Libraries in cooperation with the Center for Latin American Studies, 1968. An unannotated, but extensive, bibliography of books and articles in English and Spanish. Has sections on each country and on Latin American and Central American parties in general.

Rabinovitz, Francine, et al. *Latin American Political Systems in an Urban Setting: a preliminary bibliography.* Gainesville, Fla.: Center for Latin

American Studies, Univ. of Florida, 1967. Unannotated bibliography of 434 books and articles published since 1960 in English, Spanish, Portuguese and French. Includes sections on "Political Culture and Attitudes" and "Intergovernmental Relations." Intended "as an aid both to those interested in the study of the political systems of Latin America and those concerned with the new field of comparative urban development."

Behrendt, Richard F. *Modern Latin America in Social Science Literature*. Albuquerque, N.M.: Univ. of New Mexico Press, 1949. "A selected, annotated bibliography of books, pamphlets, and periodical articles in English in the fields of economics, politics, and sociology of Latin America."

Humphreys, R. A. *Latin American History; a guide to the literature in English*. New York: Oxford Univ. Press, 1958. Descriptive listing of over 2,000 books and articles on the history of Latin America, arranged by country. Brief section on "Politics, Government and Law" under each country.

Peraza, Fermin. *Revolutionary Cuba; a bibliographical guide*. Coral Gables, Fla.: Univ. of Miami Press, 1966–   . An annotated list of 695 books and pamphlets published in or about Cuba during 1966. Includes both English and Spanish-language monographs; a separate annual publication listing periodical articles is planned. *Revolutionary Cuba* is a continuation, in English rather than Spanish format, of the *Anuario Bibliografico Cubano,* which appeared from 1937 through 1965.

Reason, Barbara, et al. *Cuba Since Castro; a bibliography of relevant literature*. Washington: Special Operations Research Off., American Univ., 1962. Unannotated listing of about 180 items, chiefly periodical articles, with emphasis on the 1959–1962 period. Put together quickly by SORO after the Cuban missile crisis "as a support service to the Army as well as to research groups and to others likely to require guidance to the post-Castro-influence literature on Cuba."

Harvard University Library. *Latin America and Latin American Periodicals*. 2 vs. Cambridge: Harvard Univ. Press, 1966. (Widener Library Shelflist, No. 5.) Lists over 25,000 books and 1,600 periodicals on Latin America in the Harvard libraries. Separate listings by author, date of publication, and the Library's classification system.

Zimmerman, Irene. *A Guide to Current Latin American Periodicals; humanities and social sciences.* Gainesville, Fla.: Kallman Publishing Co., 1961. Lists and annotates several hundred periodicals in all fields, arranged by country and subject. Has a four-page section listing and evaluating political science journals.

Einaudi, L. and H. Goldhamer. *An Annotated Bibliography of Latin American Military Journals.* Santa Monica, Calif.: Rand Corporation, 1965. "Compiled to facilitate the study and understanding of Latin American military establishments." Reprinted in the Spring, 1967, issue of *Latin American Research Review.*

Kidder, F. E. and Allen D. Bushong. *Theses on Pan American Topics.* 4th ed. Washington: Pan American Union, 1962. Unannotated listing of over 2,200 doctoral dissertations on Latin America accepted by U.S. and Canadian universities during the period 1869–1960. A later listing covering 1961–1965 appears as a supplement to the Spring, 1967, issue of *Latin American Research Review.*

Okinshevich, Leo. *Latin America in Soviet Writings; a bibliography.* 2 vs. Baltimore: Johns Hopkins Press for the Lib. of Congress, 1966. One volume covers the years 1917–1958, the other 1959–1964. Together they list about 9,000 books and articles published in the USSR on Latin America. Covers all subjects, with extensive sections on "Politics and Government," "Foreign Relations," and "Military Affairs."

OTHER REFERENCE SOURCES

Statistical Abstract of Latin America. Los Angeles: Center of Latin American Studies. Univ. of California at Los Angeles, 1955– . Compiled largely from official statistical publications of the UN, OAS, and various Latin American governments. A convenient source for data on population, social conditions, economic production, etc.

Busey, James L. *Latin American Political Guide.* 10th ed. Colorado Springs, Colo.: The Printed Page, 1966. Very brief survey of political developments in each country. Useful as background for a first course on Latin American politics, but the student will quickly go beyond it.

Sable, Martin H. *Master Directory for Latin America.* Los Angeles: Latin American Center, Univ. of California at Los Angeles, 1965. A directory of organizations and associations "with relevance and interest in Latin America." Includes sections on governmental organizations, political parties, and communications media.

Veliz, Claudio, ed. *Latin America and the Caribbean; a handbook.* London: Anthony Blond, 1968. Part I contains concise articles, by specialists, on each country of the region; each article has a brief bibliography plus some statistical data. Part II, on Latin American Political Affairs, has thirteen articles on party systems of Latin America, the military in politics, foreign relations, and other topics. Other parts cover social, economic and cultural affairs.

South American Handbook. London: Trade and Travel Pubns., Ltd., 1924– . An annual handbook with brief descriptive information on each country. Some statistical and directory information, but mainly a handbook for the tourist.

Schneider, Ronald M. and Robert C. Kingsbury. *An Atlas of Latin American Affairs.* New York: Praeger, 1965. Brief descriptive and historical information and maps of Latin American countries.

Harrison, John P. *Guide to Materials on Latin America in the National Archives.* Washington: National Archives and Records Service, 1961. List and description of records, particularly those of the State Department, relating to Latin America and which are available to scholars in the National Archives. Much of this material for the years prior to 1929 is now available on microfilm.

Hilton, Ronald. *Handbook of Hispanic Source Materials and Research Organizations in the United States.* 2nd ed. Stanford, Calif.: Stanford Univ. Press, 1956. Lists and describes major research collections of Latin American materials in the U.S. Can be updated to some extent through the *Latin American Research Review.*

U.S. Library of Congress. *National Directory of Latin Americanists.* Washington: Govt. Printing Off., 1966. Biographical data on over 1,500 social science and humanities specialists on Latin America.

U.S. Library of Congress. *Index to Latin American Legislation, 1950 through 1960.* Boston: G. K. Hall, 1961. A two-volume index, by country and subject, of the laws, decrees, etc., of twenty Latin American countries. The index is kept up-to-date in the Law Library of the Library of Congress.

Jackson, William V. *Library Guide for Brazilian Studies*. Pittsburgh, Pa.: Univ. of Pittsburgh Press, 1964. Very brief section on political science materials. Has a "Union List of Selected Brazilian Periodicals in the Humanities and Social Sciences" in over 60 U.S. libraries.

Levine, Robert M., ed. *Brazil: Field Research Guide in the Social Sciences*. New York: Inst. of Latin American Studies, Columbia Univ., 1966. A collection of articles on resources and problems of field research in Brazil, "intended largely for the use of advanced graduate students and others with academic interest in Brazilian studies . . ." Has chapters on "Political Science," "Public Administration," and "Foreign Relations."

WESTERN EUROPE

The postwar plunge into "area studies" has led to a bibliographical paradox. These studies have emphasized developing areas at the expense of Western Europe, once almost the exclusive focus of American political scientists engaged in comparative work. Partly as a result of this trend, partly as a result of the assumption that American students have better command of French, German and other European languages, there are comparatively few English-language bibliographies and reference works on the countries of Western Europe, aside from Britain. The listing below is limited to English-language sources and therefore is highly selective; there are many other sources which the advanced student, or any student who can read German, French, etc., would find useful and essential.

BIBLIOGRAPHIES

European Cultural Center. Geneva. *The European Bibliography*. Leyden: A. W. Sijthoff, 1965. An annotated bibliography of about 2,000 books, mostly published between 1945 and 1964, "dealing with Europe as a cultural entity, as a union to be created, or as a field of specific research." Has sections on "Federalism" and "Politics and Law."

Council of Europe. Council for Cultural Cooperation. *Books Dealing with Europe: bibliography for teachers*. Strasbourg: Council of Europe,

1965. Selective, annotated bibliography of books and pamphlets on European politics, history and other subjects.

Atlantic Studies. Boulogne-sur-Seine: The Atlantic Inst., 1964– . A semiannual, annotated listing of research planned or in progress on countries of the Atlantic area. Covers "political, economic, military and arms control, social, juridical and cultural relations and coordination of policies among the Atlantic countries, on their relations with the developing nations, and on their relations with the socialist states." Also has a section on recently published works.

U.S. Department of State. Bureau of Intelligence and Research. Office of External Research. *External Research: Western Europe, Great Britain, and Canada*. Washington: Department of State, 1958– . An annual listing of current social science research by private scholars and academic organizations. Has a section on Western Europe in general and on each country, with sub-sections on "Government and Politics" and "Foreign Relations."

U.S. Library of Congress. *Introduction to Europe; a selective guide to background reading*. Washington: Govt. Printing Off., 1950. An annotated bibliography of English-language books and articles on the various countries of Europe. A general bibliography covering all subjects, with sections on "The Postwar Political and Economic Scene." A *Supplement* published in 1955 covers the years 1950–1955.

U.S. Library of Congress. *The United States and Europe; a bibliographical examination of thought expressed in American publications*. Washington: Lib. of Congress, 1948–1950. "Intended to provide a key to American thought on Europe and on United States foreign policy concerning Europe." An annotated listing of books and articles on the European situation generally and in each country. Unfortunately discontinued with the 1950 volume, but covers the critical formative period of American postwar foreign policy toward Europe.

Palmer, John. *Government and Parliament in Britain; a bibliography*. 2nd ed. London: Hansard Society for Parliamentary Government, 1964. A brief bibliography of books on "The Constitution," "Parliament," "Political Parties" and related subjects. May be supplemented by Anthony Barker, "Parliamentary Studies, 1961–65; a bibliography and comment," in the July–September, 1965, issue of *Political Quarterly*. This lists recent books and articles on the British Parliament and politics generally, with emphasis on relations between the House of Commons and the Executive.

Olle, James G. *An Introduction to British Government Publications.* London: Assn. of Assistant Librarians, 1965. An excellent discussion of the availability and use of British government publications. Describes the various types of Parliamentary records and publications of government departments.

Block, Geoffrey D. M. *A Source Book of Conservatism.* London: Conservative Political Centre, 1964. Part I is a bibliography of books, articles, and official documents dealing with the Conservative Party. Part II is a series of brief "Studies in Party History."

Pemberton, John E. *How to Find Out About France; a guide to sources of information.* New York: Pergamon Press, 1966. A general guide, but has brief sections on Government," and "Society and the Press" which will serve as an introduction to sources for the student new to the subject.

Meyriat, Jean. *Political Science, 1950–1958.* New York: Cultural Center of the French Embassy, 1960. (French Bibliography Digest, Series II, No. 32.) A survey of French writing on political science for these years, with annotations in English.

Gournay, Bernard. *Public Administration.* New York: Cultural Center of the French Embassy, 1963. (French Bibliographical Digest, Series II, No. 28.) Survey of writings on public administration in France from 1944 through 1958.

Wiener Library. London. *After Hitler; Germany, 1945–1963.* London: Vallentine, Mitchell for the Wiener Lib., 1963. An unannotated bibliography of over 2,600 books and pamphlets on postwar Germany, with emphasis on politics and government. Sections on "Germany Under Occupation," "The Problems of Berlin," "The Federal Republic," etc., as well as a section listing reference books and bibliographies.

Scandinavian Political Studies. New York: Columbia Univ. Press, 1966– . A yearbook published by the political science associations of Denmark, Finland, Norway, and Sweden. Each annual volume contains substantive essays on general topics in political science and on specific studies of Scandinavian politics. A section on "Recent Political Developments" summarizes political and electoral activity in each country and contains some statistical data on elections. Each volume also has a "Summary of Political Research in Scandinavia" and a classified bibliography of writings on Scandinavian politics by native and foreign specialists.

Julkunen, Martti and Anja Lehikoinen. *A Select List of Books and Articles in English, French and German on Finnish Politics in the 19th and 20th Century*. Turku, Finland: Inst. of Political History, Univ. of Turku, 1967. A largely chronological listing of about 900 books and articles, with an author index.

OTHER REFERENCE SOURCES

Calmann, John, ed. *Western Europe; a handbook*. New York: Praeger, 1967. The latest general survey of the area, with emphasis on political matters. Part I is a concise survey of political, social, and economic patterns of contemporary Western Europe. Part II contains 26 essays by specialists on various topics. Part III deals with the many organizations relating to European integration.

European Yearbook. The Hague: Martinus Nijhoff for the Council of Europe, 1955– . Each yearbook has several substantive articles on current European matters; articles in other languages have English summaries. There are extensive summary and documentary sections on the Council of Europe and other regional organizations, plus an annual bibliography of books, articles, and pamphlets on European integration.

Europa Yearbook. London: Europa Pubns., 1959– . Part II of Volume I has descriptive and statistical information on each European country, with sections on "Political Parties and The Press," plus directories of government officials and diplomatic representation in each country. Part I of Volume I is on "International Organization," and Volume II covers Africa, the Americas, Asia and Australasia.

The Atlantic Community Quarterly. Baltimore: Atlantic Council of the United States, 1963– . Each issue has substantive articles on the Atlantic area and U.S.-European relations, plus a "Source Material" section containing texts of major statements by governments and political leaders.

Palmer, Michael and John Lambert. *A Handbook of European Organization*. New York: Praeger, 1968. Concise summaries of the structure and activities of the major European organizations: Council of Europe, NATO, European Economic Community, etc. Has membership lists and brief bibliographies.

Weil, Gordon L., ed. *A Handbook on the European Economic Community*. New York: Praeger, 1965. Background information and important documents on the EEC. Stresses economic factors, but touches on political implications.

Mueller, Bernard. *A Statistical Handbook of the North Atlantic Area*. New York: The Twentieth Century Fund, 1965. Presents comparative statistics on eighteen countries of Western Europe, plus Canada and the U.S. Emphasis is on economic data. Designed to supplement *Europe's Needs and Resources* and *The New Europe and Its Economic Future*, also issued by The Twentieth Century Fund.

Britain; an official handbook. London: Her Majesty's Stationery Off., 1948/49– . An annual handbook containing descriptive and statistical information on the government, economy, society, press, etc., in Britain. Each volume has a selective bibliography of books.

The House of Commons. London: The Times, 1945– . Published following each general election. Contains biographies of members of the Commons, plus county and borough election statistics and election manifestoes of the Labour, Conservative and Liberal parties.

Wilding, Norman and Philip Laundy. *An Encyclopedia of Parliament*. 3rd ed. New York: Praeger, 1968. Contains concise articles arranged alphabetically on the history, procedure, structure, and work of parliamentary institutions in Britain and the Commonwealth. Appendices carry chronological lists of parliamentary officers and government ministers, plus brief bibliographies.

Abraham, L. A. and Hawtrey, S. C. *A Parliamentary Dictionary*. 2nd ed. London: Butterworths, 1964. Similar to Wilding and Laundy but briefer and limited to the British Parliament. Intended for the general reader but useful to the student unfamiliar with British parliamentary practice and terminology.

Dod's Parliamentary Companion. London: Business Dictionaries, Ltd., 1832–   . An annual handbook with biographies of members of the Lords and Commons, recent election statistics in brief, and an extensive list of government officials. The British equivalent to the American *Congressional Directory.*

Ford, Percy and Grace Ford. *A Guide to Parliamentary Papers; what they are, how to find them, how to use them.* Oxford: Blackwell, 1955. Concise instructions on how to find a way through the maze of Parliamentary materials. The Fords also have published a series of "select lists" and "breviates" of parliamentary papers, which include useful abstracts of the most important papers and reports from 1833 through 1964.

Lane, John C. and James K. Pollock. *Source Materials on the Government and Politics of Germany.* Ann Arbor, Mich.: Wahrs Publishing Co., 1964. Contains translations of official documents, statements, major court decisions and other materials relating to study of German politics and government. Has sections on the background and establishment of the Federal Republic, government institutions, the federal system, political parties, and interest groups.

Chapter 17

World
Communism

There is a voluminous literature on world communism which is not wholly or specifically related to the Soviet Union or other communist countries. Chapter 9 of this guide on "English-Language Translations of Foreign Sources" and the parts of Chapter 16 on the USSR and China contain references useful for the study of communism in those countries. This chapter will cover additional sources relating to communism in general.

BIBLIOGRAPHIES

Hammond, Thomas T. *Soviet Foreign Relations and World Communism; a selected, annotated bibliography of 7,000 books in 30 languages.* Princeton: Princeton Univ. Press, 1965. Easily the most comprehensive bibliography on the subject. Part I covers "Soviet Foreign Relations." Part II is on "World Communism by Regions and Countries," and Part III covers "Special Topics," e.g., ideology, propaganda, espionage, front groups, etc. Also has a bibliography of bibliographies.

Kolarz, Walter. *Books on Communism; a bibliography.* London: Ampersand, 1963. Annotated bibliography of "some 2,500 publications in English on the development of Communism in the USSR and China and in all the principal countries of the world." Has a chronological listing of U.S. government publications on communism since 1945.

U.S. Senate. Committee on the Judiciary. Internal Security Subcommittee. *World Communism; a selected annotated bibliography.* Washington: Govt. Printing Off., 1964. Published in two parts as Senate Document No. 69, 88th Congress. Lists about 3,100 books, articles, and other sources, with primary arrangement by area and country and secondarily by subject. Covers literature up through September, 1963. Prepared by the Library of Congress for the Internal Security Subcommittee.

Pundeff, Marin. *Recent Publications on Communism; a bibliography of non-periodical literature, 1957–1962.* Los Angeles: Research Inst. on Communist Strategy and Propaganda, Univ. of Southern California, 1962. An unannotated listing of about 900 books and pamphlets, arranged geographically.

Lachs, John. *Marxist Philosophy; a bibliographical guide.* Chapel Hill: Univ. of North Carolina Press, 1967. A descriptive and critical guide to over 1,500 books and articles on the philosophy of Marx and Marxism-Leninism, including writings relating to government.

Bibliography of the Communist Problem in the United States. New York: Fund for the Republic, 1955. A comprehensive bibliography of "literature relating to Communism in the United States since the birth, in 1919, of the first American parties adopting the Communist label." A companion volume, *Digest of the Public Record of Communism in the United States,* is a comprehensive collection of federal and state statutes, administrative regulations, and court decisions on the subject. Part III is an annotated bibliography of government publications on communism. A revised and updated edition of this bibliography, edited by Joel Seidman, is scheduled for publication in 1969 by the Cornell University Press.

Delaney, Robert Finley. *The Literature of Communism in America; a selected reference guide.* Washington: Catholic Univ. of America Press, 1962. Annotated listing of about 1,700 books and documents, primarily relating to communism in the United States. A 65-page section on "Official Anti-Communist Publications" lists and annotates Congressional hearings and other documents.

U.S. Department of the Army. *U.S. National Security and the Communist Challenge; the spectrum of East-West conflict.* Washington: Department of the Army, 1961. Annotated bibliography of books and articles published during 1958–1960 relating to world communism and American security.

Lauerhass, Ludwig. *Communism in Latin America; a bibliography.* Los Angeles: Center of Latin American Studies, Univ. of California at Los Angeles, 1962. "Designed to present a relatively comprehensive list of materials published between the end of World War II, and December, 1960, dealing with the general subject: Communism in Latin America, 1945–1960." Unannotated list of books and articles, arranged by country. May be supplemented and brought up-to-date by Martin H. Sable and M. Wayne Dennis, *Communism in Latin America; an international bibliography, 1900–1945, 1960–1967.* Los Angeles: Center of Latin American Studies, Univ. of California at Los Angeles, 1968.

Uyehara, Cecil H. *Leftwing Social Movements in Japan; an annotated bibliography.* Rutland, Vt.: Tuttle, 1959. An extensive bibliography of Japanese sources. Covers all left-wing movements, with a section on Japanese communism.

OTHER REFERENCE SOURCES

Drachkovitch, Milorad M. ed. *Yearbook on International Communist Affairs, 1966–* . Stanford, Calif.: The Hoover Inst., 1967– . Intended as a "comprehensive, continuing publication in English on the international political activities of the various communist parties." Contains ten sections, the major one entitled "Profiles of Individual Communist Parties," which presents concise data on the organization, membership, domestic activities, international views, etc., of each party. A "Documentary Section" carries English versions of the major pronouncements and speeches of various parties and leaders. Other sections include a chronology of events during the year, a summary of major international communist conferences, a review of activities of leading front groups, biographies of prominent international communist figures, and a brief bibliography of books and articles.

Griffith, William E. *The Sino-Soviet Rift; analyzed and documented.* Cambridge: M.I.T. Press, 1964. Reproduces and analyzes the most important documents in the Sino-Soviet dispute up to late 1963. May be updated by Griffith's *Sino-Soviet Relations, 1964–1965* (MIT Press, 1967), which carries the analysis and documentation up to late

1965. The English-language propaganda periodical, *Peking Review,* has carried all the major polemical documents, both Chinese and Russian, in the dispute.

Dallin, Alexander. *Diversity in International Communism; a documentary record, 1961–1963.* New York: Columbia Univ. Press, 1963. A collection of major documents of the Sino-Soviet argument and other trends in international communism.

Gittings, John. *Survey of the Sino-Soviet Dispute; a commentary and extracts from the recent polemics, 1963–1967.* London: Oxford Univ. Press, 1968. A translation and commentary on 138 major Soviet and Chinese documents published since mid-1963, when open polemics began between the two parties. The Appendix includes 23 of the most important documents from the period 1950–1962, plus a "Checklist of Major Documents in Sino-Soviet Polemics, 1963–1967," which cites English-language versions of many documents not produced in this volume.

U.S. Department of State. Bureau of Intelligence and Research. *World Strength of Communist Party Organizations.* Washington: Department of State, 1950– . An annual official assessment of the strength of the communist movement throughout the world, "including information on communist voting strength, parliamentary representation, and estimated or claimed communist party membership in each country."

U.S. Congress. House of Representatives. Committee on Un-American Activities. *World Communist Movement; selective chronology, 1818–1957.* Washington: Govt. Printing Off., 1958– . A detailed chronology with reference to sources. Volume One, covering 1818–1945, was published in 1961 as House Document 245, 87th Congress. Volumes Two and Three, covering 1946–1953, appeared in 1964 as House Document 356, 88th Congress. Subsequent volumes will bring the chronology up through 1957.

U.S. Congress. House of Representatives. Committee on Un-American Activities. *Cumulative Index to Publications of the Committee on Un-American Activities, 1938–1954.* Washington: Govt. Printing Off., 1962. "A cumulative index to individuals, publications, and organizations referred to in printed hearings and reports of the committee for the years 1938 through 1954." A *Supplement* covers the period 1955 through 1960. The two indexes together run to 1,907 pages. There is a similar index for hearings of the Internal Security Subcommittee of the Senate Judiciary Committee.

Sworakowski, Witold S. *The Communist International and Its Front Organizations; a research guide and checklist of holdings in American and European libraries*. Stanford, Calif.: Hoover Inst., 1965. A list of books and pamphlets by and about the Comintern and its front groups which are held by major American and European libraries.

Degras, Jane T., ed. *The Communist International; 1919–1943: Documents*. New York: Oxford Univ. Press, Three volumes, containing translations of the most important documents and statements of the Comintern.

Chapter 18

Interlibrary
Loan

This chapter is intended only for the serious student. Since only very serious students will have read this far, however, such a warning probably is unnecessary.

In carrying out a literature search employing the methods and materials described in this guide, you may discover that your library does not have many of the books, articles and documents turned up in bibliographies, indexes, and other reference sources. The usual and in many cases the best response to this situation is to make do with whatever is available locally. Searching and researching must stop somewhere, and the student who exhausts the resources of any reasonably adequate library should have a well-documented paper.

The matter is relative to locale and purpose, however. If you are a Harvard student and have access to that university's vast library resources, making do in this fashion is one thing. It may be something else again at Podunk U. (According to the latest statistics on academic libraries, Harvard has 7,245,321 volumes; the smallest college library listed has 4,325 volumes.) If you are doing a routine term paper, you probably can get by with very little in the way of bibliographic support, but a doctoral candidate writing his dissertation may find even Harvard's library inadequate.

Whatever the impetus, it is not too much of a distortion to say that you can borrow all the materials you need from some library somewhere in some form. To do so you will need three things:

persistence, time, and money. And the more you invest of the first two, the less of the third will be needed.

Virtually every college or university library has a department or section or person responsible for "interlibrary loan," a mechanism through which they can borrow materials from other libraries. The first problem in using this service may be to establish your credentials. Some large universities restrict borrowing to faculty members and graduate students, and if you are an undergraduate you may find the door shut. Lean on it. If you make a sufficient nuisance of yourself, plead with the librarians involved, or get some professor to certify that you need to borrow materials from other libraries, you will find that library bureaucracies, though often imposing, are porous and human.

The next problem will be to find out which library has the book, periodical, etc., you want to borrow. Most reference and interlibrary loan librarians take considerable pride in their ability to perform such detective work, and they can ease this problem for you. The more you can do on your own, however, the better, and the two most important sources are:

Union List of Serials in Libraries of the United States and Canada. 3rd ed. New York: H. W. Wilson, 1965. This is an alphabetical list of over 150,000 periodicals and serials, with symbols indicating which libraries have a given title and which volumes they hold. Covers only periodicals which began publication before 1950. *New Serial Titles,* issued monthly and cumulated annually by the Library of Congress, lists periodicals and serials which began publication after 1950 and shows which libraries have them.

National Union Catalog, 1956– . A listing, by author, of books received by some 400 American libraries. Issued monthly by the Library of Congress, with periodic cumulations. Generally, the books listed were published after 1956. Publication has just begun on a retrospective *National Union Catalog* series which will include pre-1956 material.

There are many other "union lists" and "union catalogs" for the holdings of libraries in particular states or regions of the country, as well as lists of the holdings of various foreign libraries.

In recent years, because of rising demands, some libraries have been forced to cut down on lending of their materials, particularly periodicals. At the same time, however, photocopying equipment has become available which makes it possible to copy articles or sections of books at minimum cost. This practice has grown so in recent years that it has become a matter of legal and political controversy among publishers, librarians, and educators, but the student can ignore it. In using the indexes described earlier in this guide, you may come across articles not available in your own library. Through using the *Union List of Serials* or other sources, however, it should be possible to find a nearby library which has the journal you need and either to borrow it or pay them to make photocopy of the article you want.

Postscript

Finally, there are several reference sources which may be useful to the student approaching graduation and who is trying to plan ahead:

Harwood, Michael. *The Student's Guide to Military Service*. New York: Meredith, 1968. Contains a discussion of student deferments, how to obtain same, plus tips on how to live with the military if you can't avoid it.

Brownstein, S. C. and M. Weiner. *How to Prepare for the Graduate Record Examination*. New York: Barrons Educational Series, 1967. One of a number of handbooks which purport to prepare the student for the general GRE. Gives examples of questions but carries no money-back guarantee.

How to Pass Graduate Record Examination Advanced Tests: Governernment. New York: Cowles Educational Corporation, 1968. Focuses in on the special advanced test required in some cases for political science graduates.

Graham, Jane, ed. *A Guide to Graduate Study Programs Leading to the Ph.D. Degree*. 3rd ed. Washington: American Council on Education, 1965. Purpose is "to assist the prospective graduate student and his adviser in planning for advanced study and in taking the initial steps toward selecting a graduate school." A listing, by universities, of Ph.D. programs offered. For political science, indicates sub-fields offered by a department, very brief statement of requirements, size of faculty, and number of graduate students.

Cartter, Allan M. *An Assessment of Quality in Graduate Education.* Washington: American Council on Education, 1966. The most authoritative of several recent sources which attempt to "rate" graduate departments. On pages 40–41, the forty-odd "leading" political science departments are rated by quality of graduate faculty and by effectiveness of graduate program.

Grant Data Quarterly, Los Angeles: Academic Media, Inc., 1967– . "A journal devoted to the collection and dissemination of grant information and opportunities." Four issues, with each revised once a year: I—Selected Overview of Grant Support; II—Government Support Programs; III—Business and Professional Organization Support Programs; IV—Foundation Support Programs. Each issue has a section on political science possibilities.

The second and third of the sources listed above may be of some help in preventing the necessity of recourse to the first, and thus making the other sources relevant for the student, but don't count on it. The best preventive medicine is good grades along the way, for which good term papers and reports are necessary, and to which it is hoped this guide may make some small contribution.
Good luck.

AUTHOR AND TITLE INDEX

Index

McKechnie, Thomas and Carl Beck. *Political Elites*, 115

MacKenzie, Norman, ed. *A Guide to the Social Sciences*, 94

McNeal, Robert H. *Stalin's Works*, 154

Magazines for Libraries, Bill Katz, ed., 98

Maghreb Digest, 85

Mahar, J. Michael. *India*, 163

Maichel, Karol. *Guide to Russian Reference Books*, 152

Main Street Politics, Charles Press, 124

Mansergh, Nicholas, ed. *Documents and Speeches on British Commonwealth Affairs, 1931–1952*, 150

Mansergh, Nicholas, ed. *Documents and Speeches on Commonwealth Affairs, 1952–1962*, 149

Manual on the Use of State Publications, Jerome K. Wilcox, 64

Marburger, Harold J. *Texas Elections, 1918–1954*, 75

Maron, Stanley, et al. *Annotated Bibliography for Pakistan*, 164

Mars, David and H. George Frederickson. *Suggested Library in Public Administration*, 121

Marxist Philosophy, John Lachs, 193

Mason, Bruce B. *Arizona General Election Results, 1911–1960*, 74

Mason, John Brown, ed. *Research Resources*, 95

Master Abstracts, 99

Master Directory for Latin America, Martin H. Sable, 184

Materials for the Study of Federal Government, Dorothy C. Tompkins, 103

Matthews, Daniel G. *A Current Bibliography on Ethiopian Affairs*, 175

Matthews, Daniel G. *A Current Bibliography on Sudanese Affairs, 1960–1964*, 175

Matthews, Daniel G. *The New Afro-Asian States in Perspective, 1960–1963*, 148

Matthews, Donald R. *North Carolina Votes*, 75

Maxwell, Robert, ed. *Information USSR*, 155

Mayntz, Renate. "The Study of Organizations," 115

Merritt, Richard L. and Stein Rokkan. *Comparing Nations*, 72

Metropolis, D. Halasz, 125

Metropolitan America, 125

Metropolitan Area Annual, 128

Metropolitan Area Problems, 125

Metropolitan Communities, 125

Metropolitan Politics, Charles Press, 124

Meyriat, Jean. *Political Science, 1950–1958*, 188

Michigan Index to Labor Union Periodicals, 27

Middle East, 175

Middle East and North Africa, 102, 179

Middle East Journal, 175

Middle East Record, 179

Middle East Social Science Bibliography: Arab countries of the Middle East, 1955–1960, 175

Mideast Mirror, 179

Military Balance, 144

Military Manpower Policy, 136

Military Roles in Developing Countries, Peter B. Riddleburger, 137

"Military Sociology," Kurt Lang, 134

Military Year Book, S. P. Baranwal, ed., 169

Miller, Hope, et al. *A Selected Bibliography on Unconventional Warfare*, 136

Miller, William R. *Bibliography of Books on War, Pacificism, Nonviolence and Related Studies*, 138

Mississippi Election Statistics, 1900–1967, F. Glenn Abney, 75

Mitchell, Brian R. *British Parliamentary Election Results, 1950–1964*, 76

Mizan; USSR-China-Africa-Asia, 82

Modern Latin America in Social Sci-

Sable, Martin H. *Master Directory for Latin America,* 184
Sable, Martin H. and M. Wayne Dennis. *Communism in Latin America, an international bibliography: 1900–1945, 1960–1967,* 194
Safire, William. *The New Language of Politics,* 101
Saigon Press Analysis, 85
Sarkar, Bidyut Kumar. *A Selected and Annotated Bibliography of the Government, Politics, and Foreign Relations of India,* 164
Scales for the Measurement of Attitudes, Marvin E. Shaw and Jack M. Wright, 117
Scammon, Richard M., ed. *America at the Polls,* 73
Scammon, Richard M., ed. *America Votes,* 73
Scandinavian Political Studies, 188
Scarrow, Howard A. *Canada Votes,* 76
Schattschneider, E. E., et al. *A Guide to the Study of Public Affairs,* 103
Schmeckebier, Laurence F. and Roy B. Eastin. *Government Publications and Their Use,* 49, 140
Schneider, Ronald M. and Robert C. Kingsbury. *An Atlas of Latin American Affairs,* 185
Schwarz, Urs and Laszlo Hadik. *Strategic Terminology,* 144
Science, Technology, and Public Policy, Lynton K. Caldwell, ed., 105
Seckler-Hudson, Catheryn. *Bibliography on Public Administration—Annotated,* 122
Segal, Ronald. *Political Africa,* 178
Select Bibliography: Asia, Africa, Eastern Europe, Latin America, 147
Select Bibliography of Soviet Publications on Africa in General and Eastern Africa in Particular, 1962–1966, Ladislav Venya, 173
Select Bibliography on International Organization, 1885–1964, G. P. Speeckaert, 132
Select Bibliography on Traditional and Modern Africa, Peter C. W. Gutkind and John B. Webster, 170
Select List of Books and Articles in English, French and German on Finnish Politics in the 19th and 20th Century, Martti Julkunen and Anja Lehikoinen, 189
Selected and Annotated Bibliography of Books and Periodicals in Western Languages Dealing with the Near and Middle East, Richard Ettinghausen, 176
Selected and Annotated Bibliography of the Government, Politics, and Foreign Relations of India, Bidyut Kumar Sarkar, 164
Selected Bibliography of Articles Dealing with the Middle East, 176
Selected Bibliography of Materials in State Government and Politics, James Herndon and Charles Press, 122
Selected Bibliography on Interlocal Governmental Cooperation, 124
Selected Bibliography on Unconventional Warfare, Hope Miller, et al., 136
Selected Bibliography on Values, Ethics, and Esthetics in the Behavioral Sciences and Philosophy, 1920–1958, Ethel Albert and Clyde Kluckhohn, 115
Selected List of Books and Articles on Japan in English, French and German, Hugh Borton, 166
Selected Rand Abstracts, 133
Selections from China Mainland Magazines, 83
Selective Bibliography on State Constitutional Revision, 123
Serial Set, 46
Serials for African Studies, 172
Shannon, Jasper B. *Presidential Politics in Kentucky, 1824–1948,* 75
Sharma, Jagdish. *Indian National Congress,* 164
Shaw, Marvin E. and Jack M.